The Pleasures of Afternoon Tea

The Pleasures of Afternoon Tea

Angela Hynes

HPBooks
a division of
PRICE STERN SLOAN
Los Angeles

© 1987 by Angela Hynes
Published by HPBooks
a division of Price Stern Sloan, Inc.
360 North La Cienega Boulevard
Los Angeles, California 90048
Printed in the U.S.A.
12 11 10 9 8 7 6 5 4

**Library of Congress Cataloging in
Publication Data**

Hynes, Angela.
    The pleasures of afternoon tea.

    Includes index.
    1. Afternoon teas. 2. Tea.
TX736.H96   1987   641.5'3   87-275
ISBN 0-89586-579-3

Dedication

To my mother, Irene Hynes

Credits

Photography/Ken Wong
Food Styling/Dierdra B. Bugli
Prop Styling/Stephanie Puddy

Acknowledgments

I would like to thank the following people without whose help and professional expertise this book would not have been possible: Jack Artenstein and Q. Pearce at RGA; Paul Clauser, Elaine Woodard and Jan Thiesen at HPBooks; editor Becky LaBrum; Lillian Hatton at The Tea Council of the U.S.A.; photographer Ken Wong and his assistant Jamie Shaw; food stylist Dierdra B. Bugli and her assistants Jim McCardy and Bertha Amaya Franco; and prop stylist Stephanie Puddy. A very special thanks goes to Chris Dunstan for allowing us to use her wonderful Cheshire Cat Bed and Breakfast Inn in Santa Barbara, California to take our pictures, and to her staff George Mari and Carol Ryder for smiling through the disruption. Also, a word of appreciation to the following for loaning their precious belongings as props: Col. and Mrs. Stuart Brady, Mary Fenimore, Christine Holvick, Pauline Sharp and Thelma Simmons.

Contents

Tea can be presented almost anywhere in this lovely transportable teapot since the contents are held to a fine serving temperature. Freshly baked Welsh Batch Scone, page 70, redolent of spices and lightly accented with raisins and dates, beckons a generous buttering-up and perhaps a touch of homemade Amber Marmalade, page 152; delightfully chewy Cranberry Oatmeal Cookies, page 83, are an equally inviting accompaniment along with a fragrant and warming cup of tea.

Afternoon Tea

"Afternoon tea." To an expatriot Englishperson like myself, these words bring back home like no others.

They evoke photographs in the *London Times* society pages of ladies in picture hats and white gloves, sipping tea on the lawns of Buckingham Palace. They bring back memories of Earl Grey tea and wafer-thin salmon sandwiches on a more modest suburban lawn, the scent of full-blown roses and the hum of bees in the air; fluffy scones, strawberry jam and clotted cream at a thatch-roofed Devonshire tearoom; wedges of Victoria sponge cake and slabs of shortbread with giggling girl-friends at a "tea-leaf reading" session around the fire on a dark December afternoon. Last but not least, I recall escorting visiting American friends (with great relief!) to tea at the Ritz Hotel after a blistering day of sightseeing and shopping in the West End.

Thank God for tea! What would the world do without tea!—how did it exist? I am glad I was not born before tea.

Sydney Smith, *Lady Holland's Memoir*

In recent years, as Americans in increasing numbers have adopted this gracious custom, many American tourists have taken tea at the Ritz—or at the Savoy, Fortnum and Mason, Harrods or Claridge's. Taking tea has become fashionable, and its exponents are not limited to blue-rinsed ladies in need of reviving after sales at Saks. From business executives to young homemakers, everyone is finding afternoon tea an elegant way to entertain. Smart hotels in New York and Los Angeles started the trend, and it has spread like butter on warm crumpets to hotels and restaurants across the rest of the country.

Though taking tea may be the latest in chic in the 1980s, it is by no means a totally new phenomenon in the United States: its popularity has waxed and waned over the years. In fact, tea drinking has had quite a checkered history throughout the world.

The Start of Something Big

The Chinese are credited with discovering tea as a beverage some 4,000 years ago. As legend goes, Emperor Shen Nung, known as the "Divine Healer," drank only boiled water after observing that those who took this extra step fell sick less often. One day he fueled his fire with wood from a tea bush and a few tea leaves accidentally fell into the pot. The emperor found the aroma so beguiling that he drank the water despite the extra ingredient, and the rest is history.

The Indians explain the origin of tea in another way. A holy man named Darma decided to prove his faith by staying awake for seven years to meditate on Buddha. However, after only five years he began to feel sleepy! In desperation, he chewed on some leaves from a nearby bush—a tea bush, as it happened—which stimulated him to stay awake for the remaining two years. But because Darma *ate* rather than *drank* the tea, I believe the title of "first tea-drinker" still belongs to Shen Nung.

Tea was introduced to Europe in the 16th century, when Portuguese merchants established the port of Macao as a base for buying silks, spices and other Eastern exotica. A variety of goods, including tea, were shipped to Lisbon, then transported by Dutch traders to other European cities. Eventually, the Dutch cut out the Portuguese middlemen, forming the Dutch East India Company to trade directly with the Orient via Indonesia.

In Europe, both France and Germany had brief flings with tea-drinking, but the beverage soon fell from favor—the French went back to their wine, the Germans to their beer! By the mid-1600s, only England and Russia had really taken to the drink, with Holland a distant third. (Interestingly, the Dutch are still the only tea-drinking population of any size in continental Europe.)

On the preceding pages: Afternoon tea, arranged before the fireplace on a chilly winter's day, is one of life's more civilized and relaxing experiences. Toasted English Muffins, page 56, split and served with whipped butter balls and a light honey, are the inviting prelude to the glorious Grapefruit Meringue Tart, page 91, standing tall atop a pedestaled cake plate. Conclude this mellowing interlude with a glass of sherry, which is a perfectly acceptable teatime accompaniment.

Houses of Repute

When tea began to gain a British following in the 17th century, both coffee and chocolate were already common drinks. A great many coffee houses (to which only men were admitted) had sprung up in London and other major cities—and it was at these houses that tea-drinking also began in earnest. Along with a cup of tea or coffee, one could buy a pipeful of tobacco and converse with like-minded gentlemen on the arts, political issues of the day and other subjects beyond the ken of womenfolk!

In the 17th and well into the 18th century, coffee houses were great spawning grounds for literature. Writers such as Daniel Defoe and Henry Fielding had their favorite haunts;

Samuel Johnson, a self-confessed "hardened and shameless tea-drinker," had his own house—the Essex Head Club.

It wasn't just literature that emerged from these establishments. When Henry Lloyd opened a coffee house for men who worked in the shipping business, the famous Lloyds of London insurance concern was born.

A number of traditions still with us today originated in coffee houses. The first ballot box was used at the Turk's Head to settle an argument. The venerable custom of tipping also began as part of coffee house culture: many such establishments had a box where patrons deposited small change as bribes for the waiters "to insure promptness."

Some of the most well-known names in the English tea business began their rise to prominence in the early 1700s. Tom's Coffee

When friends come over for an afternoon—or perhaps an evening—of board games, lightly spiced and powdered sugar-bedecked Eccles Cakes, page 121, *and a fragrant cup of tea provide welcome fortification midpoint through play.*

House was owned by one Thomas Twining, who in 1706 began a tea dynasty that is now in its ninth generation. Robert Jackson, a grocer, established the empire that's still one of the most respected names in teas. And let's not forget Mr. Fortnum and Mr. Mason—two gentlemen who met around 1707 and later opened a marvelous food emporium that still serves one of the best afternoon teas in the city of London.

An early sales pitch for tea was a flyer put out by a Thomas Garway, advertising "the excellent and by all physitians approved China drink called by the Chineans tcha, by other nations tay, alias tee." Even back then, "doctor-recommended" was apparently a popular advertising slogan!

As a side-note, when I was a child members of my family often referred to tea as "cha"—as in "what you need is a nice cuppa cha" or "let's brew up a pot of cha." I always thought the word was Northern English dialect; it was only after I began studying the subject that I realized we had been calling tea by its classic Chinese name. The word must have been handed down through the generations in that little pocket of the country.

Royal Tea

But back to the 17th century. While the men were sipping tea in coffee houses, the women of the family were also adopting the drink on their own ground. Just as Princess Diana and Sarah Ferguson set fashions with their wedding gowns today, the bride of King Charles II was the arbiter of taste back then. Catherine of Braganza, a Portuguese princess, had married the popular monarch when he was restored to the throne after the demise of the dreary Oliver Cromwell. Catherine brought the custom of tea-drinking to the English court—and Charles, who had lived in exile in Holland, was already a devoted imbiber. After years of puritanical rule by the

"Roundheads," the English public was only too happy to copy the style of this glamorous couple, and tea-drinking entered the national consciousness.

In the mid-1700s, the tea craze gave rise to "tea gardens." These were magnificently landscaped gardens—Vauxhall and Ranelagh were among the most famous—where the fashionable would gather to take tea, share gossip, and see and be seen. Tea was served all day long from breakfast onward; in the evening, there was often entertainment.

A second important 18th century development was the formation of the Honorable East India Trading Company. With the founding of this company, England began dealing in tea directly with the East; British business con-

cerns established the first commercial tea plantations in the Assam province of India, where tea became (and remains) a major crop.

By the end of the 1700s, tea gardens had lost much of their popularity. Tea-drinking became much more of an "at-home" activity, and afternoon tea as we now know it came into being. The custom is credited to Anna, Duchess of Bedford. At that time, the day's three meals were a heavy breakfast, a light lunch and a large dinner around eight or nine o'clock. The Duchess used to complain of feeling faint around five o'clock; to ward off that familiar late afternoon sinking feeling, she started serving tea with assorted sandwiches and small cakes.

This aristocratic tea with its dainty snacks was quite different from the "high tea" served around the same time in working class homes. The latter was a hearty meal consisting of cold meats, cheeses and bread, eaten when the men came home from the factories or fields.

Teashops & Tea Dances

As the population shifted to the cities after the Industrial Revolution, the urban teashop came into existence. The first is thought to have been started by a woman proprietor of the Aerated Bread Company (ABC) in London. At first, she simply invited regular customers into the back of the shop for "a spot of tea," but the idea was so well received that she soon turned afternoon tea into a profitable enterprise. The idea was furthered by Mr. J. Lyons, who opened a corner shop in London to provide a fast, cheap tea for shop and office workers. His patrons were served by nimble-footed waitresses known as "nippies." Both the ABC and Lyons teashops soon became chains, as ubiquitous in England today as McDonald's and "Kentucky Fried" in the United States. And around the time that these two shops got underway, elegant hotels also instituted daily afternoon tea for their patrons.

The 1930s saw the heyday of another manifestation of the tea craze: tea dances. Held in ballrooms, town halls and hotels, they drew hundreds of young people on weekend afternoons. An entrance fee of about 30 cents bought tea, sandwiches and cakes, and a chance to dance to the music of the big bands popular at the time. Interestingly, tea dances have enjoyed a renaissance in modern England. Those same 1930s revelers, now enjoying their retirement, are apparently finding tea dances an ideal way to kick up their heels in their golden years.

At every level of English society, afternoon

tea has become an established ritual, unstoppable by acts of God or man. During World War II, the British government saw to it that factories were provided with tea—despite shortages—to keep up the workers' morale. And even today, it's well-known that everything stops for tea. An American friend of mine who worked briefly in a large London office was highly amused by the "tea lady" who pushed a cart through the corridors of the building at 3:30 every afternoon. Though the tea was compliments of the firm, she also sold cookies and chocolate bars to those who wanted a snack with their cuppa. During a weekend at Blackpool, a large resort town on the Lancashire coast, the same friend was puzzled by a strange daily event: around 3:30, everyone picked up their belongings and fled the beach as though a whistle had blown somewhere. That, of course, was the time all the small hotels and boarding houses set out afternoon tea in their lounges—and no matter how beautiful a day it was on the beach, tradition dictated that tea must be taken!

Tea in America

But what about the history of tea in America? At first, tea-drinking here followed much the same course it did in Europe. The Dutch established tea-drinking in New Amsterdam; the British continued the trend after purchasing the city and renaming it New York. The New World copied the old to the extent of building tea gardens and naming them for the English originals: downtown Manhattan had gardens every bit as elegant as those on the banks of the Thames, and New York City had several "tea water pumps." Even the Quakers gave the nod of approval to the sober, alcohol-free beverage.

Americans became huge tea drinkers. In the 10 years before the Revolution, a population of barely 1-1/2 million drank over 7,800,000 gallons of the brew. All of that changed when George III caused a little fracas with his taxes, culminating in a tea party at Boston that was not at all the type of party we are talking about in this book! We'll skip quickly over that unsavory incident: suffice it to say that tea-drinking was renounced by all true American patriots at that time, and it's been a long haul back.

There have, however, been some notable patriots who did not take the tea sanction too seriously. According to his biographers, George Washington drank it "all day and night." Abraham Lincoln loved tea and held a men-only tea party the very Sunday before he was elected. More recently, Dwight D. Eisenhower was a tea drinker; so was John Kennedy, who enjoyed a cup in his office every afternoon.

America has made two big contributions to tea-drinking—both, I'm afraid, regarded as sacrilegious by true tea buffs. The first is iced tea, invented at the Louisiana Purchase Exposition in 1904. When a heat wave caused fair-goers to bypass the tea exhibition in search of cold drinks, Richard Blechynden—representing Indian tea growers—poured his brew over ice in order to compete with the lemonade stands. This bit of Yankee ingenuity (albeit devised by a visiting Englishman) started quite a trend: about three-quarters of all tea drunk in the United States today is iced.

The second contribution, also dating from 1904, was the teabag. It started as a marketing gimmick by Thomas Sullivan, a New York tea merchant, who sent customers samples of his wares in little silk pouches. To his surprise, orders began to pour in for tea packaged this way as people discovered how convenient it was to pour boiling water over the bags.

As the 20th century has progressed, tea-drinking has gathered momentum in America. Consumption has doubled in the last decade, and Americans now drink around 46 billion servings a year.

Afternoon Tea Today

Across the country, from the Plaza Hotel in New York to the Mayfair Regent in Chicago, from Dallas's Adolphus to trendy Trumps in Los Angeles, tea is booming. Between three and six o'clock in the afternoon, tearooms are alive with the swish of crisp white linen and the chink of silver against fine china.

When one thinks about it, it's only logical that afternoon tea should become the newest and most fashionable meal of the day: tea is a tradition that's ideal for the 80s. For the fitness-conscious, tea is a luxurious, relaxing, yet allowable replacement for heavy lunches, after-work drinks and elaborate dinners. The beverage itself is soothing and nonalcoholic and, while many traditional tea accompaniments are rich, portions served are small. *Kaffeeklatsches* and cocktail parties are out—and afternoon tea is definitely in.

The executive set, too, have adopted afternoon tea with enthusiasm. A tea break provides a calm oasis in a frantic, stress-filled schedule—and ending the day over a fragrant pot of tea in a quiet tearoom is far more relaxing than battling up to the bar in a smoky cocktail lounge. In addition, the tearoom is a discreet and formal setting for meetings. It's a place where both men and women can feel comfortable—an important consideration today when more and more women hold executive positions.

Now it's time to start serving afternoon tea at home. It's a gracious yet inexpensive way to entertain, a truly versatile meal that offers the adventurous host or hostess ample opportunity for creativity. Tea can be formal or casual, intimate or crowd-size, served indoors or out, a light snack or a substantial meal. The food is enjoyable to prepare and a delight to present. The traditions, the etiquette, what to serve, how to serve—everything you need to know about afternoon tea is in this book.

Afternoon Tea For All Occasions

Though he was an American, Henry James captured teatime beautifully in this line from *The Portrait of a Lady*: "There are few hours in life more agreeable than the hour dedicated to the ceremony known as afternoon tea."

That fact has long been a well-kept secret among the English. Even when you are not entertaining others, the ritual of teatime can be a welcome and very civilized break in a busy day. There's a lot to be said for the solitary tea: try it, and treat yourself as elegantly as you would guests. In the late afternoon, stop whatever you're doing and steal half an hour for yourself. Brew a fragrant pot of tea—do not dunk a teabag!—and arrange some light sandwiches and a cookie or a small cake on a pretty plate. Carry your tray to a favorite place—a window seat, a sofa before the fireplace, perhaps a secluded corner of the garden. Take the opportunity to catch up on letter writing, cuddle your cat or simply reflect on the day. After a few sips of "the cup that cheers," the world will seem a calmer place. Agreeable indeed!

It's just as much fun to have unplanned afternoon tea if a friend drops by unexpectedly. The beauty of tea is that you can

Exotic travels? Handsome strangers? Abundant wealth? What will the future bring? According to devotees, it's all in the tea leaves.

rustle up the food quite easily from ingredients you probably keep on hand in your kitchen: flour, butter, eggs, milk, sugar. A batch of oven scones, for example, takes only about 15 minutes to make from scratch. Eat them at the kitchen table while they are fresh and warm from the oven. Or have a simple farmhouse tea, with slices of crusty bread, butter and jam, fresh fruit—and, of course, several cups of good strong tea.

I remember many such spontaneous and congenial teas in my own home. My mother used to "read" tea leaves—tell fortunes by the configuration of leaves in the bottom of the cup. She poured the tea from pot to cups without using a strainer. After the tea had been drunk, the drinker would swirl the dregs around the cup three times clockwise, then turn the cup upside down on the saucer. After the last drops of tea had drained out and the leaves were spread around the side of the cup, my mother would tell of impending letters, tall dark strangers or other good news. Though she insisted her fortune-telling was all in fun and that she made it up as she went along, friends who used to drop by for a "reading" were certain she had some kind of power!

You might consider learning the rudiments of tea-leaf reading from one of the books available in the library, or find someone in your neighborhood who is adept at it. It's a great form of entertainment to provide at your tea party.

"Nursery" Tea

In middle- and upper-class English homes, it was once quite common for children to be raised on a day-to-day basis by a nanny (remember Mary Poppins?). The young children had tea before the nursery fire in the early evening, after being bathed and just before bedtime. This was often the hour when parents spent time with their children. "Tea," in this instance, might consist of a soft-boiled egg in an egg-cup, fingers of bread or toast and cups of cocoa for the children, and toasted muffins or scones and fragrant tea for the adults.

That era is long gone, and we are now in another age when both parents often work all day and family get-togethers are difficult to arrange. If this is the case in your household, try having an occasional "family" (rather than "nursery") tea when everyone comes home at day's end. Tea food, after all, is the stuff kids love: buns, cookies, cakes. They can help bake the scones and toast the crumpets. Perhaps family tea can become a whole new tradition in your home.

Entertaining with Tea

As opposed to the impromptu teas described above, an arranged tea party should be planned like any other party. Start making the arrangements and sending invitations several weeks in advance of the date. Because many of your guests may not have been to an afternoon tea in a private home before, and may therefore be unsure of the protocol, be specific with your invitation. Give a definite time—"four o'clock" not "four-ish"—just as you would for a cocktail party, and put an endpoint to the tea—"four to six." This helps avoid the embarrassing situation of guests lingering well into the evening.

That hour about which James waxed poetic can be anywhere between three and six o'clock in the afternoon. The general rule is that the earlier tea is served, the lighter the refreshments. At three, tea is usually a snack—dainty finger sandwiches, petits fours, fresh strawberries; at six, it can be a meal—or "high" tea—with sausage rolls, salads and trifle. You can serve high tea around the dining room table, but afternoon tea is more of a living room occasion, with everything brought in on a tray or cart. When the days are cold, the den is a perfect place for tea; in summer, you can take tea on the patio or in the garden.

Tea is a meal for all seasons; it's also suitable for all occasions. Here are a few ideas on when and how to give a tea party.

The Intimate Tea

So you thought afternoon tea was just for "the girls"? Not at all! Tea with a lover can be most charming and romantic. If you are not convinced, picture this scenario:

It's a blustery Sunday afternoon in winter. You and the man in your life have just come home from the football game, chilled to the bone and ravenous. While he gets the fire blazing, you rustle up tea. You choose robust, smoky Lapsang Souchong, a perfect foil for the weather. As you snuggle up on the sofa, the drapes closed against the darkening evening, you dig into toasted crumpets all dripping with butter, and rich, spiced fruit cake.

When the teapot runs dry, you pour two glasses of sherry, possibly Harveys Bristol Cream—yes, that's allowable!—as you finish off your cherry tartlets. Your teatime is a cozy prelude to a warm winter's evening.

Or this:

The two of you have spent a wonderful summer's day antique-hunting in back lanes. As the sun begins to slide westward down the sky, you sit in the garden at a table covered with a pretty tablecloth and decorated with an informally arranged bowl of fragrant lilacs.

The spread is further enhanced by a mound of fluffy scones and pots of jam and sweet country whipped cream.

The tea is Earl Grey, an aromatic, flower-scented blend. You also serve glasses of crisp dry champagne to make this an *occasion*. As you nibble on fresh raspberries, you admire the silver teaspoons that were your big find of the day.

I'm sure you get the picture. But apart from being cozy and romantic, tea for two has other advantages. The food is simple and easy to prepare, so you don't have to worry about something going drastically wrong at the last minute to spoil the mood. And tea provides an unintimidating way to invite a new man friend to your home. The occasion is informal—and, unlike a late-night date, an afternoon tea has a clear endpoint.

Here are some tips to enhance the intimacy of your tea *a deux*.

- Use your best china. Teacups and saucers are always preferable to heavy mugs. Don't worry if you haven't inherited the family Royal Doulton—any pretty china will do. If you are planning to entertain this way regularly, though, you might consider investing in a small tea service, usually consisting of a teapot, milk pitcher, sugar bowl, six teacups and saucers and six cake plates.

- Use cloth napkins—linen or cotton. Paper napkins just don't cut it on romantic occasions!

- Present the food attractively. Cover your tray or teacart with a tray cloth, doilies or a pretty napkin. A single rose in a bud vase, a little jug full of daffodils or a small basket of seasonal fruit can add warmth to the scene. Alternatively, make the food itself the centerpiece by arranging your sandwiches, cookies and cakes on an old-fashioned, three-tiered cake stand.

- When it comes to food, anything goes. Because there are only two of you, you can chance sticky, crumbly or dripping dishes which would be a messy disaster if passed among more people.

Informal Tea Parties

An informal tea is an intimate, fun way to entertain up to about 10 people. Of course, you don't need a reason for entertaining friends, but many occasions offer the perfect excuse for throwing a tea party. In fact, afternoon tea might be just what you need to add a little pizzazz to some occasions that have become stale and predictable.

- Be the first on your block to have a bridal or baby tea shower. The traditional time for showers—usually early evening after work—is ideal for a tea party.
- If you have a regular crowd over to play cards or a board game, surprise them by serving afternoon tea instead of the usual coffee fare.
- Serve tea when you have a Tupperware or lingerie party.
- Revive the weary parents at your child's birthday party by serving tea—in another room, away from the noisy horde of kids!
- Shock the men by serving tea when you join them to watch the game on television. They just might find it a pleasant change from pizza and pretzels.

Atmosphere is an important part of the afternoon tea ritual. Hold your informal tea party in the den or living room. In winter, light a crackling fire; all year-round, decorate the room with seasonal flowers. Keep music quiet and melodic rather than intrusive. Many famous tearooms have a pianist or harpist playing in the background, and that type of music seems to go especially well with the chink of china. In warm spring or summer weather, it's perfectly fine to host your tea party on the lawn or patio.

Bring the refreshments in on trays or a wagon and set them out on a table so guests can help themselves. You, as hostess, should pour the tea, passing it to each guest in turn. You'll need a teapot and an additional kettle of hot water for "topping up," a tea strainer and small dish to deposit the tea leaves in, a pitcher of milk, a small plate of lemon slices, sugar and artificial sweetener, teacups, teaspoons, small plates, cake forks and napkins. In this instance, pretty paper napkins are perfectly fine if you don't have enough cloth napkins to go around.

When it comes to food, you have quite a range of choices. With only 10 guests or fewer, your party is small enough for everyone to be seated and to eat with a fork. Serve a selection of sandwiches; freshly-baked scones; tea specialties like Chelsea buns; cookies, small cakes or tartlets; and a large cake or tart as a centerpiece. You might also serve ice cream or a light dessert such as Almond Crème (page 126). Or serve all of the above! One of the delightful advantages of afternoon tea is that you can produce a veritable "groaning board" with remarkably little expense.

Picnic Tea

A picnic provides a perfect occasion to serve afternoon tea. Imagine enjoying that still, golden light of late afternoon on the beach or in a meadow, with a sumptuous tea spread out on a quilt. Or have a tailgate picnic out of a wicker hamper while you savor nature's autumn foliage display.

The only difficulty involved in presenting an afternoon tea *al fresco* is finding a way to make freshly brewed tea with boiling water. The problem is solved if you have a camping stove or plan to picnic where you are permitted to build a fire. Pack into your picnic basket a measured amount of loose tea in a tea ball, and boil your water in a kettle or covered pan. When the water comes to a boil, remove it from the flame and immediately drop the tea ball into the water. Cover the kettle or pan, infuse and serve the tea in the usual manner (see page 30).

In the event that you're unable to boil water at the picnic site, try this thermos bottle method. First, make a pot of tea in the usual manner at home. When it has infused, strain it into a thermos and close tightly. Do not add sugar, milk or lemon; carry those items separately and add to the tea when serving. Though the tea purist might wince at this technique, it does give a perfectly fine cup of tea. In any case, avid picnic fans know that everything tastes better out-of-doors.

Picnic food should be finger food—neat to eat, easy to pack and serve. Sandwiches tend to get soggy if wrapped too long, but other savories such as Scotch eggs and Cornish pasties are perfect. Slices of loaf cake, cookies and individual tarts also work well. Set the food out buffet-style on your picnic blanket. Your guests need only a supply of paper napkins— no plates or silverware.

Formal Tea Receptions

A tea reception can be held on more formal occasions, or when the guest list grows too long for everyone to gather around together. Instead, guests stand or circulate while eating. Such a tea is a novel way to celebrate any family get-together; on the less personal side, it's also ideal for a committee meeting, business open house, church social or fund-raiser.

This type of occasion requires more formal organization than does an informal tea, and the hostess will need some assistance in serving. It works best to utilize two rooms. Have the tea and food laid out buffet-style in one location, such as the dining room, patio or kitchen, and let the guests help themselves. They then move out to the living room or garden to enjoy the light repast.

On one end of a long table, or on a separate small table or credenza, set out a teapot containing a tea concentrate (recipe on page 30), a large pot or kettle of hot water, a pitcher of milk, a plate of lemon slices, sugar and artificial sweetener, teacups and teaspoons. Station someone here to help pour the tea concentrate and top it up with water, and to replenish both as they run dry. For a celebration, you might also serve one of the tea-based punches on pages 36-37.

The food table should have small plates and a good supply of paper napkins at one end. If the table is long or if you're hosting a large number of guests, position plates and napkins at both ends so that guests can serve themselves more quickly. An elegant centerpiece can make your table look stunning. Use candles, seasonal flowers and foliage, a grouping of plants, an arrangement of fruit or vegetables—whatever is appropriate for the occasion and sets the mood. The food should then be arranged attractively on the table around the centerpiece.

Stick to food that can be eaten with the fingers; crumbly, floppy or sticky foods are difficult to eat standing up. Similarly, keep it bite-size. It's well-nigh impossible to juggle a plate, a knife or fork and a cup of tea all at the same time. Despite these limitations, you still have a wide range of foods to choose from. Sandwiches and other small savories such as cheese straws and—if you feel extravagant— caviar puffs work well. Round out the spread with an assortment of cookies, colorful petits fours, fruit tartlets and hearty loaf cakes cut in thin slices. Pretty dishes of nuts, mints and candies placed around the rooms can also supplement the meal.

Here are some ways to make your tea reception run smoothly:

- ☙ For groups of more than 25 guests, try to have someone passing through the crowd with trays of finger food in addition to the buffet spread.
- ☙ Strategically place piles of paper napkins around the room for emergencies.
- ☙ Assign a friend or family member to scoop up used cups, plates and napkins as soon as they are discarded. Nothing spoils the elegance of the occasion as quickly as piles of dirty dishes cluttering up the room.

High Tea

High tea is distinct from afternoon tea in that it is usually a much more substantial offering. Still common in many parts of England, it is traditionally the meal eaten when the men return from work and before the young children go to bed. (The adults also have a light supper later in the evening.) Weekday high teas are generally kept to the immediate family, but on weekends and holidays the meal becomes a social affair with friends or extended family coming by.

Because high tea is an early evening meal, it's an ideal way to celebrate when you have guests of all ages to consider: It's perfect for the youngsters as well as the elderly. Think about hosting a high tea for a special wedding anniversary, a graduation or a family reunion. And what about holidays? Halloween, Easter and Christmas Eve all lend themselves to the idea with traditional cakes or other dishes forming the centerpiece.

High tea should be a "sit-down" meal served around the dining table, so limit the number of guests to as many as you can comfortably accommodate. Arrange place settings as you would for a meal with silverware, bread plates, dinner plates and cloth napkins.

During the week, high tea usually consists of a fairly simple meal of leftovers, cold cuts, salad, bread and butter, a tart or cake and perhaps a light dessert like fruit and gelatin. When you're entertaining guests, a much more elaborate meal is appropriate. Serve the heartier savories like Cornish pasties, Scotch eggs and sausage rolls, with chutneys and relishes as well as salads. Replace mundane bread and butter with crumpets, muffins, pikelets or delicious homemade tea breads, accompanied with sweet butter and preserves or honey. Tarts, cakes and perhaps a trifle complete the meal.

The "Power" Tea

With "power" lunches and "power" breakfasts common parlance among the executive set, can "power" tea be far behind? This elegant manner of conducting business is becoming quite chic in the United States. At many of the top hotels where tea is served, it's the business people who arrive in droves in late afternoon to conclude their deals over cups of vintage Darjeeling. (In England, serving tea at office business meetings has long been standard practice.)

If you decide to hold a power tea, remember that classy accouterments are of prime importance: a matching china tea service; perhaps a silver teapot; a good, stain-free linen tray cloth and napkins. Serve a good-quality loose tea and keep the food plain—your business associates aren't going to want sticky fingers if they are handling papers. A selection of sandwiches and some simple pastries are perfect choices.

And more power to you!

The Recipes

While it's true that there are many excellent restaurants in England, we English are not generally renowned for the quality of our cuisine. We've stoically lived with charges of tasteless boiled vegetables, overcooked meat and stodgy puddings for years, unable in all conscience to refute them. But we can hold our collective heads high in the kitchen because there are two occasions when British cooking comes into its own: breakfast and tea.

The great British breakfast with mounds of scrambled eggs, great Scottish kippers, deviled kidneys, bangers bursting their skins, rashers of meaty bacon, tomatoes, mushrooms, fried bread and gallons of the ever-present tea is outside the scope of this book. Suffice it to say that when friends visit England, I always recommend they stoke up in the morning and don't eat again until teatime. That way, they come back thinking English food is wonderful!

Teatime food is indeed wonderful. The French may be masters of the subtle sauce, the Italians pasta perfectionists, but the English are the bakers of Europe. Baking, of course, is at the heart of the tea table. The aroma of home-baked cakes, scones, pies and cookies wafts over the land around four o'clock in the afternoon. Where you are determines what scent will greet you. For a country that's so small geographically, England offers a surprising abundance of regional specialties.

It has always seemed to me that in the United States you write songs about cities and towns. Every time I arrive in a city, be it by

A classic silver tea service, polished to a fare-thee-well, adds elegance to afternoon tea. The traditional set includes a teapot, a hot water kettle over a burner, plus creamer, a covered sugar, and a bowl for emptying any dregs from the first cup of tea. On a less formal note, a cup of tea, Shrewsbury Cookies, page 76, and a good book can have a most pleasant effect on the psyche.

plane or automobile, I involuntarily start humming a tune. Chicago, Kansas City, New York, Detroit, St. Louis, and so forth—all evoke popular songs. But in England we name food after our towns! In the following pages you'll find recipes named for Bath, Chelsea, Eccles, Dundee and many others. It seems that almost every city and hamlet has found reason to invent a bun or pie.

In fact, many regional recipes are quite similar, with only minor differences—and different names, of course. What is called a crumpet in the southern half of the country, for example, is often called a pikelet in the north. Eccles cakes, Chorley cakes and Banbury cakes are all essentially mixtures of dried fruits and spices wrapped up in pastry, but all three towns lay claim to the recipe. When recipes are so similar, I have included only one version; in this instance, you will find a recipe for Eccles cakes on page 121.

Traditional recipes from the south of England, where the climate is warmer and summer sunlight lasts until about 10 in the evening, tend to be a little lighter than those from the north and Scotland. The south is famous for its berry crops and its orchards: for instance, the county of Kent is known as "the garden of England." Crisp apples, sweet cherries, fragrant pears and luscious peaches provide fillings for tarts, pies and cobblers.

The northern counties have less clement weather. Winter nights draw in around three o'clock and recipes are more substantial, often making use of such ingredients as oatmeal, dried fruits and spices. Scotland, the most northerly country of the British Isles, offers a particularly rich bounty of teatime and traditional treats, many of which contain a "wee dram" of something to add a warming kick!

The ubiquitous scone deserves a special word. A very old tradition, it is still an essential element of afternoon tea. Every area of the country has its own version of the scone or griddle cake. Yorkshire has its havercakes, Scotland bannocks and Shropshire jannocks, and the Isle of Man takes pride in its dumb cakes. Perhaps the most captivating name belongs to a scone from the Newcastle area—the "singin' hinnie." Because of its high fat content, this scone tends to sputter and hiss—"sing"—as it cooks on a hot griddle.

Today, for convenience, individual scones are almost always made with a cookie cutter and baked in the oven. However, until early in this century, they were more commonly cooked in a single large round, then cut into wedges. And in general, they were cooked over direct heat, usually on a griddle. A typical griddle was a flat cast-iron plate, usually 12 to 14 inches across, with a curved handle like that you'd see on a basket. The heated griddle was lightly greased with suet and the scone was cooked on top of it for a few minutes on each side. In parts of Scotland, Ireland and Northern England, scones were often cooked on a bakestone: a large, flat rock heated over a peat fire and used like a griddle.

Well into this century, the kitchen or parlor (living room) fire was also used for toasting breads, buns, crumpets, muffins or pikelets, while the family enjoyed afternoon tea around the hearth. The food would be speared on the three prongs of a brass toasting fork about 1-1/2 feet long and held over the flame until warmed through and crispy.

Ingredients

England's rainy climate results in lush meadows, which in turn make for great dairy country. It's no wonder, then, that many tea recipes are heavy with butter, cream and milk.

To true tea aficionados, selecting a blend is a complex and highly personal matter. Beginning with the tin on the upper left, this sampler shows just a smattering of what is available: aromatic China rose, hearty Persian black tea, full-bodied Assam, delicately flavored Japan green tea, the infamous pellet-leafed gunpowder tea, and pungently flavored Lapsang Souchong.

Numerous centuries-old traditional recipes such as syllabub, custard, trifle, blancmange, flummery and junket are cream- or milk-based puddings.

England's fertile fields also yield great crops of berries: strawberries and raspberries, of course, but also loganberries, black currants and gooseberries, all commonly found in foods eaten at teatime. The same applies to soft summer fruits: peaches, plums, apricots and cherries. In fact, England's cherry crop is so prolific that summer cherry festivals have been held since the 1400s. The cherry tartlets on page 97 are an adaptation of a very old recipe that my mother gave to me.

But even the most traditional of English recipes isn't limited to ingredients grown on that sceptered isle. From the earliest times, the British have been traders and colonists, importing no end of exotic bounty from distant lands. Tea recipes are redolent with spices and seasonings from the Far East; brown sugar, rum and molasses from the West Indies; Madeira wine from the Canary Islands; raisins and nuts from continental Europe; and dates, figs, bananas and coconut from the Middle East and Africa. These ingredients are so integral a part of the English kitchen that many cooks would probably need to be reminded that they're not really of English origin.

Teatime Accouterments

The afternoon tea parties covered in this book are not nearly as ritualistic as, say, the Japanese tea ceremony. The British sensibility is one of a more offhand charm. Nevertheless, there are touches that can make the experience a little more special, a little more authentically "English." The equipment described below will add that particular ambience to your party.

China	You're probably familiar with the classic names such as Wedgewood, Royal Doulton and Spode (the latter being the first manufacturer to add ground bone to clay, thus making "bone china"). These houses make beautiful tea services—delicate yet resilient, and certain to become heirlooms. Once you have chosen your pattern, you can collect your service piece by piece. But don't be intimidated if you don't own such a set. These days, you can buy beautiful china that's very reasonably priced and available in many department stores.
Teapots	Silver teapots (especially antiques) look absolutely elegant, but purists think they distort the flavor of the tea. China, pottery and glass give a truer taste. If you use your teapot regularly, a brown coating will develop inside the pot as a result of tea solids and hard water. Scrub it clean with any good cleanser, or use one of the products marketed for cleaning coffee pots.

Tea Cozies	These are a peculiarly English notion. A tea cozy is a cover for your teapot that helps keep the contents hot, and almost every English grandmother has a pattern for knitting them! Most look like a stocking cap with a bobble on top; two slits—one on each side—let the handle and spout poke out. More sophisticated versions are made from padded, insulated fabrics, much like oven mitts or potholders. These lack the handle and spout openings; instead they fit over the entire pot and must be removed to pour the tea.
Tea Strainers	Some teapots have a built-in strainer across the entrance of the spout. These usually don't catch all the leaves since they're typically made with quite large holes to allow the tea to pour through evenly. For more efficient straining, pour the tea through a separate strainer held over the cup. Tea strainers are traditionally made of metal and come with a matching saucer to hold the strainer on the table. If you cannot find one like this, look for the inexpensive bamboo strainers sold in most Oriental or import shops.
Tea Balls	A forerunner of the teabag, a tea ball is a perforated, ball-shaped metal container. Loose tea is clasped inside and the ball is placed in the pot or cup before the boiling water is poured in. Tea balls are not recommended for regular use as they tend to inhibit the full flavor flow of the tea. But they are convenient—and certainly preferable to a teabag!—for occasions such as picnics or for times when you want a quick cup for one.
Sugar Tongs	"One lump or two?" Sugar cubes are most commonly served at tea parties, and the hostess should drop them into the guest's cup with sugar tongs. You might have to hunt them down in an antique or collectibles shop, but these little silver tongs do add a touch of elegance to your table.
Muffin Dishes	Usually made of silver, these are shallow dishes with domed lids that you pop your muffins under as you finish toasting them. The covered dish keeps the muffins—or other breads and buns—warm at the table. Some manufacturers of fine silver make muffin dishes, or you might make a project out of finding a pretty antique.
Bun Warmers	Much more rustic than a silver muffin dish, the bun warmer is another device for keeping breads and buns warm. An unglazed ceramic tile is heated by immersing it in very hot water for a few minutes. You then dry it off and wrap it in a pretty cloth napkin or clean kitchen towel. Place it in the bottom of a basket, and it will ensure that your tea treats stay warm enough to melt butter!

There's Nothing Like A Nice Cuppa Tea

Tea, of course, is the cornerstone of an afternoon tea party. And if you're going to entertain this way, it's essential to brew a good cup of tea—golden, steaming, fragrant and refreshing. The *Encyclopedia Britannica* somewhat superciliously reports that "Americans are generally indifferent to the cup quality of tea and have slight knowledge of the different types of tea." If such an accusation is never to be leveled at you, toss out the teabags, ignore the instant, and read on.

Growing Tea

In China, Japan, India and Sri Lanka (Ceylon), tea growing has been a high art for centuries; excellent teas now also come from Taiwan, Indonesia, Bangladesh, Iran, parts of Africa such as Malawi, Kenya, Tanzania and Rwanda, and even Argentina.

Tea generally grows best at high altitudes in warm, rainy climates. Tea plantations are vast estates, their fields filled with rows of waist-high, flat-topped bushes. These bushes (*Camellia sinensis*) would reach heights of 40 feet if not cut back every few years, and each bush can produce tea for up to 50 years.

Modern technology notwithstanding, tea is still plucked by hand. Men and women walk between the rows, tossing the "flush"—the tender growing tips of the tea plant consisting of two leaves and a bud—into baskets strapped to their backs.

Varieties of Tea

Every kind of tea contains tannin, an astringent; caffeine, a stimulant; water; and an essential oil that gives it its flavor. The tea's flavor depends on a number of factors: the altitude at which the tea is grown; the growing conditions (soil composition and amounts of rainfall and sun); when the tea is plucked; and processing and blending. Like wines, teas are tested, tasted and graded by experts who rate both flavor and color, using their own descriptive vocabulary. Taste may be classified as "pungent," "pointy," "meaty," "bodied," "bakey" or "thick," and color as "coppery," "dull" or "bright." Once you start experiment-ing with teas, you will discover an infinite variety of colors and flavors that make your old teabags seem quite bland.

Teas are divided into three groups—*green, oolong* (or *semifermented*) and *black*—according to how they are prepared for market. Processing begins with *withering*, which means the tea is spread on huge racks and dried (withered) by circulating hot air. It is next crushed by rollers to release the aromatic juices, then left in a cool, moist atmosphere to ferment and, except in the case of green teas, oxidize. The oxidation process turns the tea a bright copper color and the final stage of preparation, a firing to further reduce moisture, turns the tea black. During these various processes, the amount of tannin in the tea is reduced and the flavor is enhanced.

Green Teas.

You may also hear these teas called "basket-fired" or "pan-dried." So-called because of their pale color, green teas don't undergo the oxidation process that turns tea leaves dark. Instead, a steaming process is used. Most Japan teas are green. Many others, such as Singlo, Hyson and Twankay, come from China. The most famous green tea is probably Gunpowder, which comes in the form of little pellets. Green teas tend to be light in color and delicate though astringent in taste. They are rarely drunk at afternoon tea, but it is perfectly acceptable to serve one if you or your guests have a taste for it.

Oolong or Semifermented Teas.

Oolong—the word means "black dragon" in Chinese—is produced by a combination of techniques used for green and black teas. The leaves are brown and the tea brewed from them is darker than green tea, with a characteristic aromatic flavor. Among the

---

On the preceding pages: Tea is served on the patio from an attractive, and practical, hammered pewter tea set. Flaky Cheese Straws, page 41, and deliciously chewy Coconut Mounds, page 82, are presented on elegant glass plates.

most popular varieties are Formosa Oolong, with a subtle flavor and bouquet, and Jasmine, delicately scented with jasmine blossoms.

❧ Black Teas.

The most common teas both in England and America, these are made from fully oxidized leaves and come in many varieties. Selecting black teas is a bit like selecting wines—it's worth knowing a little about the subject before you choose.

Assam. Full-bodied, rich-colored and robust, this is a high-grade India tea grown in one of the country's northeastern provinces.

Ceylon. Among the most commonly sold teas, Ceylon is generally delicate and fragrant. It is made from tea grown in Sri Lanka (formerly Ceylon) at elevations between 2,000 and 7,000 feet. The best comes from above 4,000 feet so look for the words "high grown" on the package. The district of Uva, with its dry days and cool nights, produces particularly fine Ceylon teas.

Darjeeling. This classic tea is one of the most favored of India teas. Grown in the Himalayas, it has a fine, delicate flavor and aroma. Select it if you are ever in doubt about which tea to choose—you won't be disappointed. *Vintage Darjeeling*, harvested only once a year, is quite rare and will impress a connoisseur.

Earl Grey. A sweet, citrusy tea flavored with bergamot, Earl Grey may be produced from black tea from India, Sri Lanka or China. The tea is named for one of the many Earl Greys, a good friend of a mandarin who gave him the recipe for this finest of all teas. Many manufacturers offer a version of Earl Grey. Elegant and light, it's an afternoon tea favorite.

English Breakfast. The characteristics of China tea dominate in this mellow blend of black teas. It's just as acceptable for afternoon tea as for breakfast.

Keemun. The Chinese consider mild but robust Keemun a fine tea to take with meals. A high-grade China tea originally made in the Kiangsi province, it is frequently used in breakfast blends.

Lapsang Souchong. Pungent, strong Lapsang Souchong originated in the Chinese provinces of Fukien and Hunan. Smoking over wood gives this tea its rich, unique flavor. Lapsang Souchong is definitely an acquired taste; if you serve it at a tea party, also offer a milder tea, such as Darjeeling or English Breakfast, for guests who find Lapsang a little too robust.

Pekoe and Orange Pekoe. At one time these two terms referred to a type of China tea often flavored with orange. Today, though, they more commonly describe only the *size* of the leaf, not the flavor or quality of the tea. You can buy Darjeeling Pekoes, Assam Pekoes, and so forth. The name "pekoe" tells you that you're getting the largest grade of tea, as opposed to *broken pekoes*, the smaller *fannings* and the even smaller *fines*. Most teas are made from a combination of sizes, with fannings and fines predominating in teabags and catering blends.

Prince of Wales. A hearty tea with a good bouquet, this blend of Keemun teas was first created for the Duke of Windsor. It's now a very popular afternoon tea.

In addition to the above traditional teas, you will find an enormous number of specialty teas flavored with everything from apple to licorice. Today's market offers something for every taste. There are even decaffeinated teas, though it's worth noting that a cup of regular brewed black tea has only half the caffeine of coffee (3/4 grain per cup versus 1-1/2 grains per cup).

Storing Tea

Tea tends to absorb moisture and odors, and the volatile oil to which it owes its flavor evaporates if exposed to air. Buy it in small quantities and store in airtight containers in a cool place.

Making Tea

Once you have chosen your tea (or teas), it's essential that you make it correctly to best bring out its flavor. Follow the classic method below to brew all teas, unless the package instructs you otherwise.

1. Fill your teakettle or a saucepan with fresh, cold water. Do not reboil water; this makes the tea taste "flat."

2. When the water is hot but not boiling, pour a little into a clean teapot; then return the kettle to the heat. Most tea connoisseurs prefer glass or earthenware pots since metal tends to distort the flavor of the tea. Swirl the hot water around the pot to heat it thoroughly, then throw the water away and wipe out the pot. Preheating the teapot helps keep the water at the boiling point when it's poured over the tea; a cold pot brings down water temperature.

3. Put 1 teaspoon of tea in the pot for each cup of tea. Put the lid on the pot and allow it to stand while the water finishes boiling. This helps draw the flavor from the leaves before the water is poured on.

4. Boiling water is required to bring out the full flavor of tea. When the water reaches a rolling boil, take the pot to the kettle and pour the water gently over the tea leaves. It's important to carry the pot to the kettle, not vice versa. Once removed from the heat, the water loses one degree per second—so if you take the kettle to the pot the water will no longer be at the boiling point.

5. Put the lid on the teapot and allow the tea to brew 3 to 5 minutes (or for the time stated on the tea package). Stir once during this time. Brew by the clock, not by the color, as various blends reach different intensities of brown.

6. Pour the tea through a tea strainer into cups and serve with lemon slices or milk (never cream—it curdles in tea) and sugar as desired. If you take milk in your tea, tradition dictates that it should be poured into the cup first. Adding milk before tea was originally just a means of protecting the delicate bone china teacups from the hot tea, though some people also swear it makes a difference in the taste by taking the edge off the tannin. However, you might find it easier to get the right mix if you pour the tea first, then add the milk.

7. After pouring the first round of cups, top up the pot with hot water to refresh the brew and enable a second round.

Tea for Large Parties

Making tea by the classic method just described may well be impractical if you're preparing tea for a large group. It's easier to use the following tea concentrate, developed by the Tea Council of the U.S.A., to give an excellent cup of tea with all the full flavor of a fresh-brewed cup. The recipe makes enough for about 25 servings.

1. Make tea as directed, but use 1 quart (4 cups) of water over 2/3 cup of tea leaves.

2. Let stand 5 minutes, then stir and strain into a teapot or pitcher.

3. When ready to serve, pour about 2 tablespoons of concentrate into each cup, then fill cup with steaming hot water.

The Ubiquitous Tea Bag

Up until now I have been somewhat scathing about the lowly tea bag but, if the truth be known, I have on occasion made myself a single mug of tea with one. There's a lot to be said for convenience, so why the bad reputation? The run-of-the-mill tea bag is held in

Taking the teapot to the kettle, not vice versa, is not only proper but necessary as boiling water brings out the fullest flavor in the tea.

such poor esteem among tea aficionados because the quality of tea used in bags is generally not very high. Furthermore, in many restaurants tea bags are served with a jug of lukewarm-to-hot water that does absolutely nothing to bring out what flavor there might be in the bag.

In recent years, many good tea companies such as Twining's, Bigalow's and Fortnum & Mason have vastly improved the reputation of the tea bag by packaging better qualities of tea in such flavors as Earl Grey, Darjeeling and English Breakfast. You might find this an ideal way to sample a new tea. Once you have found a tea you like, then you can buy the more expensive loose version. Be forewarned, however, that the loose tea will taste a little more robust and flavorful than the bagged

variety. The difference between tea from bags and tea brewed from loose leaves is a little like the difference between instant coffee and fresh perked.

When making tea with a bag, follow the same guidelines as you would for loose tea: warm the pot or mug, use freshly boiling water, and infuse the bag for the recommended amount of time—usually three to five minutes. Remove the bag with a spoon and allow the excess tea to drip back into the cup. Do not squeeze or wring the bag into the cup as that will result in bitter residue being deposited in your tea.

And never use a tea bag twice: all the flavor will have been used the first time. Tea made from a second-hand tea bag can only be stale and lifeless.

While purists will undoubtedly stick to traditional tea, there may be times when you'd like to serve something different. For just those occasions, here are a few tea recipes—some hot, some chilled.

Tea Julep

2 cups cold water
1/2 cup sugar
1/2 cup lightly packed fresh
   mint leaves
7 cups brewed black tea,
   chilled
Ice cubes
8 small mint sprigs

The mint adds a refreshing touch to this iced tea.

❧ In a small saucepan, combine water, sugar and mint. Stir over low heat until sugar is dissolved. Increase heat to medium and bring to a boil; boil about 5 minutes or until liquid is slightly syrupy. Remove from heat and set aside to cool. Strain into a bowl or pitcher; stir in tea. Pour into ice-filled glasses and garnish with mint sprigs. Makes 8 servings.

Mulled Tea

2-1/2 quarts (10 cups) cold
   water
6 whole cloves
13 cinnamon sticks
1/4 cup mellow black tea
   leaves such as Darjeeling
   or English Breakfast
1-3/4 cups orange juice
Juice of 2 lemons (about 1/2
   cup)
Sugar to taste

Flavored with spices and citrus juices, this tea is perfect for a winter day.

❧ In a large saucepan, combine water, cloves and 1 cinnamon stick. Bring to a boil. Place tea in a large bowl or pitcher. Pour boiling water and spices over tea. Allow to brew 5 minutes. Stir in orange juice and lemon juice. Pour mixture back into saucepan; gently reheat, but do not boil. Strain into cups or tea glasses. Sweeten with sugar and serve with a cinnamon stick. Makes 12 servings.

Mint-flavored Tea Julep rejuvenates and refreshes, even on the most scorching of days.

Iced Tea

Black tea leaves (allow 1-1/2
  teaspoons per cup)
Boiling water
Ice cubes
Sugar to taste
Lemon twists or mint sprigs

Traditionally American, a frosty glass of iced tea is a treat your guests will enjoy on a hot day.

Following the traditional method (see page 30), brew a black tea using 1-1/2 teaspoons tea per cup of boiling water. Pour brewed tea into glasses filled with ice cubes. Sweeten with sugar and garnish each serving with a twist of lemon or a mint sprig.

Russian Tea

Black China tea leaves such
  as Keemun (allow 2
  teaspoons per cup)
Boiling water
Sugar to taste
Lemon slices

This sweetened tea is usually served in a glass rather than a cup.

Following the traditional method (see page 30), brew a black China tea using 2 teaspoons tea per cup of boiling water. For each serving, half-fill a tall glass with tea; top up glass with hot water. Sweeten tea with sugar and add a lemon slice to each glass.

Variation
Stir 1 teaspoon dark rum into each glass of tea; omit lemon slices.

Apple Tea

Mellow black tea leaves such
  as Darjeeling or English
  Breakfast (allow 1
  teaspoon per cup)
Boiling clear apple juice
Sugar to taste
Cinnamon sticks

Boiling apple juice is used for brewing instead of boiling water.

Following the traditional method (see page 30), brew a mellow black tea using apple juice instead of water and 1 teaspoon tea per cup of juice. Pour tea into cups. Sweeten with sugar and serve with a cinnamon stick.

Whether taken plain, with lemon or with milk, freshly brewed tea soothes the soul and gives a marvelous lift to lagging spirits.

Apple Cider Cup

Flavored with cider and brandy, this tea is served at room temperature.

2-1/2 teaspoons black tea leaves

2-1/2 cups boiling water

1/4 cup sugar

Juice of 2 oranges (about 1 cup)

1/2 cup brandy

5 cups apple cider, chilled

8 thin lemon slices

Following the traditional method (see page 30), make tea from tea leaves and boiling water; allow to brew 5 minutes. Place sugar in a large bowl or pitcher. Strain hot tea into bowl and stir until sugar is dissolved. Stir in orange juice. Set aside to cool. Just before serving, stir in brandy and cider. Pour into glasses and float a lemon slice on each serving. Makes 8 servings.

Tea with Liqueur

Mellow black tea leaves such
    as Darjeeling or English
    Breakfast (allow 1
    teaspoon per cup)
Boiling water
Fruit-flavored liqueur such
    as Calvados, Cassis,
    Cherry Heering, Cointreau
    or Framboise
Sugar to taste

Use your favorite liqueur and serve this tea for a special occasion.

🍃 Following the traditional method (see page 30), brew a mellow black tea using 1 teaspoon tea per cup of boiling water. To serve, pour about 2 tablespoons liqueur into each cup or tea glass. Fill cups with hot tea. Sweeten with sugar.

Gin Punch

1-1/2 cups cold water
1/2 cup sugar
Juice of 6 lemons (about
    1-1/2 cups)
Juice of 6 oranges (about 3
    cups)
3 cups brewed black tea,
    chilled
1/2 (750-ml.) bottle gin
2-1/2 quarts (10 cups)
    carbonated mineral water,
    chilled

Serve Gin Punch for a summer celebration.

🍃 In a small saucepan, combine water and sugar. Stir over low heat until sugar is dissolved. Increase heat to medium and bring to a boil; boil about 10 minutes or until mixture is reduced to a thick syrup (you should have about 1 cup). Remove from heat and allow to cool. Pour syrup into a punch bowl. Stir in lemon juice, orange juice, tea and gin. Allow to stand about 1 hour. Just before serving, stir in mineral water. Makes 25 servings.

An attractive, strawberry-filled ice ring afloat in Champagne Punch keeps this mellowing refreshment properly chilled.

Champagne Punch

5 teaspoons black tea leaves
5 cups boiling water
2 cups sugar
Juice of 6 lemons (about
  1-1/2 cups)
Ice ring or ice cubes
1 (750-ml.) bottle dry red
  wine, chilled
1 (750-ml.) bottle dry white
  wine, chilled
1 (750-ml.) bottle light rum,
  chilled
1 (750-ml.) bottle
  champagne, chilled

The combination of tea and wine make a smooth punch suitable for the most special of occasions.

Following the traditional method (see page 30), make tea from tea leaves and boiling water; allow to brew 10 minutes. Pour sugar into a large punch bowl. Strain hot tea into bowl and stir until sugar is dissolved. Stir in lemon juice. Cool completely. Just before serving, add ice, then wines, rum and champagne. Makes about 25 servings.

Sandwiches & Savories

For formal and informal afternoon get-togethers, a selection of tiny sandwiches plays a supporting role to the true stars of the tea table—scones, cookies and pastries. But when it comes to a sit-down high tea, a more substantial savory spread, served with salad, takes center stage.

Traditionally, high tea savories were made of lunchtime leftovers: chopped meat, cooked vegetables and the like. Many of the recipes here reflect that heritage—but others, such as Caviar Puffs, are sophisticated and delicious in their own right and owe *nothing* to leftovers.

Savory Tartlets

1/2 recipe Short-Crust
　Pastry, page 86
3/4 cup (3 oz.) finely
　shredded Cheddar cheese
1/2 cup plus 2 tablespoons
　milk
1 egg
1/4 teaspoon dried Italian
　seasonings
1 teaspoon chopped fresh
　parsley
Salt and pepper to taste

These delicious little tarts feature an herbed cheese-custard filling. They'll remind you of quiche.

◆ Preheat oven to 350F (175C). Grease 12 shallow 2-inch tartlet pans. On a floured surface, roll out pastry with a floured rolling pin. Cut in 12 rounds with a 2-1/2-inch cookie cutter. Line tartlet pans with pastry rounds. Sprinkle each with 1 tablespoon cheese. Set aside. In a medium-size bowl, lightly beat together milk, egg, Italian seasonings, parsley, salt and pepper. Spoon into pastry shells. Bake about 20 minutes or until pastry is golden and filling is set. Carefully remove tartlets from pans and transfer to a wire rack. Cool slightly. Serve warm. Makes 12 tartlets.

Ham & Veggie Tea Bread

2 tablespoons butter or
　margarine
1 small onion, chopped
3 celery stalks, chopped
4 cups self-rising flour
Salt and pepper to taste
1/4 cup solid vegetable
　shortening, chilled, cut in
　chunks
2/3 cup milk
1 egg, beaten
3/4 cup finely chopped
　cooked ham

This is a tasty and unusual bread.

◆ Preheat oven to 375F (190C). Grease a 9" x 5" loaf pan. Melt butter in a medium-size skillet over low heat. Add onion and celery; cook, stirring frequently, about 5 minutes or until vegetables are tender. Remove vegetables from skillet and set aside to cool. Sift flour, salt and pepper into a large bowl. With your fingers, rub shortening into dry ingredients until mixture is crumbly. Add milk, egg, ham and vegetables; mix with a wooden spoon to form a soft dough. Turn out onto a floured surface and knead lightly. Shape into a rectangle and place in greased loaf pan. Bake about 1 hour or until a wooden pick inserted in center comes out clean. Turn out of pan and cool on a wire rack about 10 minutes. Cut into slices to serve. Makes 8 to 10 servings.

On the preceding pages: High tea, held in the comfort of the dining room, features an assortment of more substantial savories as well as a traditional sweet or two. Quiche-like Savory Tartlets, page 40, fresh Caribbean Scones, page 67, with plenty of butter and Amber Marmalade, page 152, and a crisp green salad are the temptations leading up to Tropical Apple Tart, page 92.

A bit of shredded Cheddar gives a golden hue to cheese straw dough, which is cut into a combination of rings and "straws." After baking the pastry, about five straws are slipped through each ring and both are arranged together on a tray for proper presentation.

Cheese Straws

1 cup all-purpose flour
Salt and red (cayenne)
  pepper to taste
1/4 cup cold butter, cut in
  small pieces
1/2 cup (2 oz.) finely
  shredded sharp Cheddar
  cheese
1 egg yolk
Cold water
Paprika

The interesting presentation makes these savories special.

Preheat oven to 400F (205C). Grease 2 large baking sheets; set aside. Sift flour into a large bowl; season with salt and red pepper. With your fingers, rub butter into flour until mixture is crumbly. Mix in cheese and egg yolk. Add enough cold water, a little at a time, to make a stiff dough. Break off 1/3 of dough and set aside. On a floured surface, roll out remaining 2/3 dough 1/4 inch thick with a floured rolling pin. Using all of this dough, cut in strips 1/2 inch wide and 3 inches long. Roll out reserved dough to same thickness. Cut in rounds with a 2-inch cookie cutter; cut out centers with a 1-1/2-inch cutter. Re-roll cut-out centers to make more straws. Transfer all straws and rings to greased baking sheets. Bake 10 to 15 minutes or until pale golden brown. Transfer to a wire rack to cool. Dust ends of straws with paprika. Divide straws evenly among rings. To serve, slip straws through rings. Makes about 8 rings and 40 straws.

Chicken liver pâté, pureed to a velvety smoothness and piped into a partially hollowed baguette, is an ideal high tea offering.

Pâté Rounds

10 ounces chicken livers
1/4 cup butter
1 large onion, thinly sliced
2 garlic cloves, sliced
2 parsley sprigs, chopped
1 (12-inch) baguette
1 tablespoon brandy or dry
  sherry
Salt and pepper to taste
Milk, if needed

A sophisticated savory for times when you want something a little more filling than traditional afternoon tea sandwiches. If you like, you can use more liquor instead of milk to soften the mixture.

Cut veins from chicken livers; discard. Set livers aside. Melt butter in a large skillet over low heat. Add onion and garlic and cook, stirring often, just until soft. Add chicken livers and parsley. Increase heat and sauté briskly 3 to 4 minutes or until livers are firm. Remove from heat and set aside to cool. Cut rounded ends from baguette. Using a long, sharp knife and a teaspoon, very carefully remove soft bread from center of loaf, leaving walls about 1/2 inch thick. Spoon chicken livers into a blender or food processor; process until mixture forms a smooth paste. Turn into a bowl; add liquor, salt and pepper. If necessary, add milk, 1 tablespoon at a time, until mixture is soft enough to drop from a spoon but too thick to pour. Spoon pâté into a pastry bag fitted with a 1/2-inch tip. Pipe pâté into loaf. Smooth ends with a knife. Wrap loaf in foil and refrigerate 1 hour. With a sharp knife, cut crosswise in slices about 1/2 inch thick. Makes about 18 rounds.

Savory Crackers

1 cup whole wheat flour
1/4 teaspoon salt
1 teaspoon dry mustard
2 tablespoons cold butter or margarine, cut in small pieces
2 cups (8 oz.) finely shredded Cheddar cheese
About 2 tablespoons cold water

Crisp and light, these crackers can be served plain or lightly spread with one of the sandwich fillings (see pages 50-51).

Preheat oven to 450F (230C). Grease 2 large baking sheets. In a medium-size bowl, stir together flour, salt and dry mustard. With your fingers, rub in butter until mixture is crumbly. Add cheese. Stir in water a little at a time to form a soft dough. Turn out onto a floured surface and knead gently until smooth. Roll out thinly with a floured rolling pin. Cut into rounds with a 2-inch cookie cutter. Place on baking sheets and prick with a fork. Bake 5 to 7 minutes or until crackers are slightly puffy and light brown. Carefully transfer to wire racks to cool. Makes about 45 crackers.

Scotch Eggs

2 teaspoons all-purpose flour
Salt and pepper to taste
4 hard-cooked eggs, shelled
1 teaspoon Worcestershire sauce
1/2 pound bulk pork sausage
1 egg, beaten
1 cup fine dry bread crumbs
Vegetable oil for deep-frying
Parsley sprigs

Scotch eggs are often served in pubs, to be washed down with a glass of beer. But they are also appropriate when you want to provide a filling snack for a high tea. Serve with green salad and a tangy chutney.

Combine flour with salt and pepper in a small bowl; dust lightly over eggs. Add Worcestershire sauce to sausage and mix well. Divide sausage into 4 equal portions. Pat each portion into a round with your hands. Place 1 hard-cooked egg in center of each round. Mold meat evenly around egg, covering completely; make sure there are no cracks in the meat. With a pastry brush, coat the meat with beaten egg; roll in bread crumbs. In a deep-fryer, heat about 4 inches oil to 350F (145C) or until a 1-inch bread cube dropped into oil turns golden brown in 65 seconds. Carefully add eggs and cook 7 to 8 minutes or until outside is crisp and golden. Drain well and cool before serving. To serve, cut each egg in half lengthwise and decorate cut side with a sprig of parsley. Makes 8 halves.

Mushroom Turnovers

3/4 cup (12 tablespoons)
   butter
1/4 cup thinly sliced shallots
2 cups thinly sliced fresh
   mushrooms
1 tablespoon all-purpose
   flour
1/4 teaspoon curry powder
1/2 cup whipping cream
Salt and pepper to taste
10 sheets frozen filo pastry,
   thawed

These tasty savories are made with filo pastry, available frozen in most well-stocked supermarkets.

Melt 2 tablespoons butter in a large skillet over medium heat. Add shallots and mushrooms; cook, stirring frequently, until soft. Reduce heat and add 2 more tablespoons butter. Stir in flour and curry powder. Cook, stirring constantly, 1 to 2 minutes. Remove from heat and stir in cream. Return to heat and stir until mixture is thickened; do not boil. Season with salt and pepper. Remove from heat and set aside to cool. Preheat oven to 375F (190C). Grease a large baking sheet; set aside. Melt remaining 1/2 cup butter in a small saucepan. Remove from heat. Working with 1 filo sheet at a time, lightly brush each sheet with melted butter. Using a sharp knife, cut filo in half lengthwise. Fold each half lengthwise and brush again with butter. Put a scant tablespoonful of mushroom mixture in 1 corner of each folded sheet; fold bottom of pastry over filling to form a triangle shape, then continue folding over and over like a flag. Place filled pastries on greased baking sheet; cover lightly. When all turnovers have been made, brush tops with melted butter. Bake 20 to 25 minutes or until puffed up and golden. Serve warm. Makes 20 turnovers.

Cornish Pasties

1-1/2 recipes Short-Crust
   Pastry, page 86 (3 cups
   pastry)
3/4 pound chuck steak,
   trimmed of fat, finely
   diced
1 large potato, peeled,
   chopped
1 small onion, chopped
Salt and pepper to taste
1 egg, beaten

These delicious little pies are often taken on picnics or packed into lunch sacks, and they are also perfect served with a green salad for high tea. Though traditionally made with an uncooked filling, as in this version, pasties may also be filled with leftover vegetables and cooked meat. In this instance, reduce the total cooking time to 20 minutes at 425F (220C).

Preheat oven to 425F (220C). Grease a large baking sheet; set aside. Divide pastry in 6 equal portions. On a lightly floured surface, roll each portion into a round about 6 inches in diameter with a floured rolling pin. Mix meat, potato, onion, salt and pepper in a medium-size bowl. Divide into 6 portions; place 1 portion to 1 side of center of each pastry round. Moisten edges of pastry with water. Fold 1 side over to form a semicircle. Press edges together to seal, then crimp with thumb and forefinger. Place on baking sheet and bake 15 minutes. Brush tops with egg. Reduce oven temperature to 325F (165C) and bake pasties 1 hour longer or until pastry is golden brown. Transfer to a wire rack to cool. Makes 6 pasties.

Mushroom Turnovers, filo filled with a mushroom, shallot and cream mixture punctuated with curry, are traditional teatime treats.

Sausage Rolls

1 sheet (14" x 11") frozen
puff pastry, thawed but
still cold
1/2 pound extra-lean pork
sausage
1 egg, beaten

A snack for all occasions, sausage rolls are served in pubs, on picnics, at cocktail parties—and, of course, for tea.

Grease a large baking sheet; set aside. Set pastry on a lightly floured surface. With a sharp knife, cut pastry lengthwise into 2 (14" x 5") strips. (Discard excess strip or reserve for decoration, if desired.) Set aside. Divide sausage in 2 equal portions. On a floured surface, roll each portion with your hands to make a 14-inch long rope. Place 1 sausage rope on each pastry strip and fold pastry over to encase meat. Moisten edges with water; press to seal. Cut each roll crosswise in 7 (2-inch) rolls. Cut 2 small diagonal slits on top of each. Place rolls seam-side down on greased baking sheet. Refrigerate 15 minutes. Meanwhile, preheat oven to 450F (230C). Brush rolls with egg. Bake about 30 minutes or until pastry is crisp and golden and meat is cooked. Transfer to a wire rack to cool. Serve warm or cold. Makes 14 rolls.

Variation
Substitute precooked sausage links for pork sausage. Lay links lengthwise on pastry. Cut between links after sealing. Bake 12 minutes or until pastry is golden.

The tri-color garnishment of black, red and golden caviar nests atop lemon-enhanced and sour cream-filled choux paste puffs.

Caviar Puffs

1/4 cup unsalted butter
1/2 cup water
1/2 cup all-purpose flour, sifted
1/2 teaspoon salt
2 eggs, lightly beaten
1-1/2 teaspoons lemon juice
About 1/4 cup dairy sour cream
2 tablespoons caviar

For an ultra-luxurious tea, impress your guests with these surprisingly inexpensive treats. You don't have to use the best Russian caviar—unless you want to, of course! Try one of the excellent varieties from California or Oregon, or use any good fish roe. In any event, you need only a small amount.

Preheat oven to 425F (220C). Rinse a large baking sheet with cold water; shake off excess water but leave sheet damp. In a medium-size saucepan, combine butter and water. Place over medium heat and bring to a boil, then remove from heat. Add flour and salt all at once and beat with a wooden spoon until blended. Return to low heat and continue beating until dough comes away from sides of pan and forms a ball. Set aside to cool to lukewarm. With a wooden spoon or an electric mixer, gradually beat eggs into dough, beating until mixture is glossy and smooth. Spoon mixture into a pastry bag fitted with a plain 1-inch tip. Pipe about 1-inch-diameter puffs on damp baking sheet, leaving room for expansion. Cover puffs with an inverted roasting pan. Bake about 35 minutes without lifting lid so pastries can cook in their own steam to make light, crisp puffs. With a sharp knife, slit each puff down 1 side to allow steam to escape. Cool on a wire rack in a draft-free area. Shortly before serving, stir lemon juice into sour cream. Fill puffs with a scant teaspoon of sour cream and top with caviar. Makes 12 to 14 puffs.

Cheese Puffs

1 (1-lb.) loaf white bread, cut in 5/8-inch-thick slices
4 egg whites, room temperature
1/2 teaspoon baking powder
Salt and pepper to taste
2 cups (8 oz.) finely shredded Cheddar cheese
Parsley sprigs

These are fine teatime treats for chilly weather, or to serve to children at a high tea. Slice the bread thicker than for tea sandwiches—about 5/8 inch thick. A 1-pound loaf should make about 12 slices. (This is also a good recipe for using up old or hardened cheese.)

Lightly grease a large baking sheet. Toast the bread; cut each slice into 4 squares. Arrange squares on baking sheet and set aside. In a large bowl, whisk or beat egg whites until stiff. Whisk in baking powder, salt and pepper. Fold in cheese. Preheat broiler. Pile cheese mixture atop toast squares. Broil 2 inches from heat 2 to 3 minutes or until golden and puffy. Cheese mixture browns quickly so watch carefully. Serve hot on an earthenware platter garnished with parsley sprigs. Makes about 48 puffs.

Curry Puffs

1 tablespoon butter
1-1/2 tablespoons all-purpose flour
1 teaspoon curry powder
1/2 cup plus 2 tablespoons milk
1 (4-oz.) package frozen shrimp, thawed, rinsed, drained, chopped
Salt and pepper to taste
1 sheet (14" x 11") frozen puff pastry, thawed but still cold
1 egg, beaten

A legacy of the old Colonial days, curry continues to be a very popular flavoring in Britain.

Preheat oven to 450F (230C). Grease 2 large baking sheets; set aside. Melt butter in a medium-size saucepan over low heat. Add flour and curry powder and stir with a wooden spoon until smooth. Continue stirring 2 to 3 minutes longer or until mixture is bubbly. Remove from heat; gradually add milk, stirring constantly to prevent lumps from forming. Return to heat and cook, stirring, until sauce boils and thickens; then cook 1 minute longer. Place shrimp in a bowl and stir in sauce a little at a time; mixture should be thick. Season with salt and pepper; set aside. Set pastry on a lightly floured surface. Cut in rounds with a 1-1/2-inch cookie cutter. Divide shrimp mixture among 1/2 of pastry rounds. Top each with remaining rounds. Moisten pastry edges with water and press lightly to seal. Crimp edges together with tines of a fork. Arrange pastries on baking sheets. Brush lightly with egg. Bake 10 to 15 minutes or until puffed and golden. Transfer to a wire rack to cool. Serve warm or cold. Makes about 40 puffs.

Afternoon tea sandwiches are traditionally very light—just fragile morsels not intended to be a meal in themselves. They are simply an elegant, savory adjunct to the other richer, sweeter offerings. Choose sandwich fillings with a delicate, but not bland, flavor; for suggestions, see pages 50-51.

To make your tea sandwiches, buy unsliced loaves of fresh, firm-textured white bread and slice the bread very thin. A 1-pound loaf cut this way should make about 16 slices. Before adding a filling, lightly spread one side of each slice to the very edges with softened butter. (When buttering very thin slices of bread, you may sometimes find it easier to spread each slice *before* cutting it from the loaf.) One-half cup (one 1/4-pound stick) of butter will spread a 1-pound loaf. For an extra-smooth sandwich spread, you may use a mixture of 1/2 cup softened butter and 1/4 cup mayonnaise, beaten together until blended.

To assemble each sandwich, spread a thin layer of filling on the buttered side of one bread slice; top with a second slice, buttered-side down. Trim off the crusts, then cut the sandwich diagonally into quarters, making four small triangles. A 1-pound loaf yields about 30 triangles. As a rule of thumb, allow about 3 triangles per person.

For variety, you may want to leave some of the sandwiches open-faced to show off the fillings. Or make pinwheel sandwiches instead of the usual triangles; these are a little more time-consuming to prepare, but they're very attractive. (Directions for pinwheels are on page 50.)

Arrange your completed tea sandwiches on a pretty plate or platter and garnish as desired. Parsley, watercress, chives, small celery stalks with leaves, stuffed olives, lemon wedges and pickles are all suitable choices.

Harlequin Fingers

1/2 of 1-pound loaf unsliced white bread
1/2 of 1-pound loaf unsliced whole-wheat bread
1/2 cup butter, room temperature
1 pound cream cheese, room temperature

These two-tone layered sandwiches make your tea presentation especially attractive.

❧ Trim crusts from both loaves. Cut bread in 1/2-inch-thick slices. Lightly spread butter and cream cheese on 1 side of each slice. Stack 4 slices, alternating white and whole-wheat bread; stack first 3 slices filled-side up, then set top slice in place filled-side down. Repeat with remaining bread slices. Wrap in foil and refrigerate at least 1 hour. To serve, cut stacks in strips about 1/2-inch wide, slicing through all 4 layers. Arrange on plate with striped side up. Makes about 30 fingers.

Afternoon tea always includes an assortment of light sandwiches. It's easy to vary the selection simply by beginning with a base of several kinds of bread, using a variety of cookie cutters and presenting them both open-faced and closed. This pleasant array features a quintet of fillings plus two-tone Harlequin Fingers enhanced with various embellishments.

Pinwheel Sandwiches

1 (1-lb.) loaf unsliced
  day-old white bread
1/2 cup butter, room
  temperature
Fillings of your choice *except*
  Salmon & Cucumber
  (suggestions follow)

Be sure to use day-old bread for these pretty sandwiches; fresh bread is too difficult to cut lengthwise.

Neatly cut off all crusts from loaf of bread. Lightly spread butter to edges of 1 long side. Cut lengthwise into as thin a slice as possible. Spread buttered side of slice with filling. Roll up lengthwise jelly-roll style. Wrap in foil. Repeat until loaf is finished; you should have about 6 rolls. Refrigerate for at least 1 hour; butter will harden and hold rolls together. Before serving, cut each roll crosswise in about 5 slices. Makes about 30 pinwheels.

Tea Sandwich Fillings

Each of the following 5 recipes—Egg & Cress, Piquant Tuna, Cream Cheese, Celery & Walnut, Golden Chicken and Salmon & Cucumber—make enough filling for a 1-pound loaf of bread.

Egg & Cress

1 small bunch watercress,
  washed, drained, patted
  dry
5 hard-cooked eggs, shelled
5 tablespoons mayonnaise
2-1/2 tablespoons Dijon-style
  mustard
Salt and pepper to taste

The watercress adds an interesting peppery taste to this sandwich.

Using a knife, coarsely chop 1/2 of watercress and set aside; you should have about 1/2 cup, lightly packed. Reserve remaining watercress sprigs for garnish. In a medium-size bowl, roughly chop eggs with a knife. Add mayonnaise and mustard; season with salt and pepper. Mash to a smooth paste with a fork. Stir in chopped watercress. Make sandwiches with egg mixture. Arrange on plate and garnish with remaining sprigs of watercress.

Piquant Tuna

1 (7-oz.) can water-packed
  tuna, drained, flaked
5 tablespoons mayonnaise
1 tablespoon lemon juice
Salt and pepper to taste
1 teaspoon capers, finely
  chopped
Whole chives

Water-packed tuna is lower in calories than tuna packed in oil.

Place tuna in a medium-size bowl and mash with a fork. Stir in mayonnaise and lemon juice; season with salt and pepper. Mash to a smooth paste. Stir in capers. Make sandwiches with tuna mixture. Garnish plate with chives.

Cream Cheese, Celery & Walnut

1 pound cream cheese, room
  temperature
1 (about 1-lb.) celery heart,
  very finely chopped
1 cup diced walnuts
Parsley sprigs

This easy-to-do filling can be made in minutes.

In a small bowl, beat cream cheese until smooth. Mix in celery and walnuts. Make sandwiches with cheese mixture. Garnish plate with sprigs of parsley.

Golden Chicken

2 hard-cooked egg yolks
1 teaspoon butter, melted,
  cooled
1 teaspoon lemon juice
1 cup minced cooked
  chicken
1 teaspoon chicken stock or
  broth
Salt and pepper to taste
Small celery stalks with
  leaves

Egg yolks add richness and color to this chicken filling.

In a medium-size bowl, mash egg yolks with a fork. Stir in butter and lemon juice. Add chicken and stock; season with salt and pepper. Mash to a smooth paste. Make sandwiches with chicken mixture. Garnish with celery.

Salmon & Cucumber

1 large English cucumber
1 (6-1/2-oz.) can skinless,
  boneless pink salmon
Salt and pepper to taste
Lemon wedges

Sandwiches made with this filling must be served at once.

Thoroughly wash and dry cucumber. With tines of a fork, deeply score cucumber lengthwise from top to bottom on all sides; wipe off loose rind with a paper towel. (Scoring in this way is an alternative to peeling that leaves some of the rind still on the cucumber for "bite" and nutrition; it also gives the cucumber a decorative scalloped edge when sliced.) Cut off and discard cucumber ends. Slice cucumber wafer thin. Place slices in a single layer on paper towels to drain. Drain salmon. Place in a medium-size bowl and mash well; season with salt and pepper. Make sandwiches with a thin layer of salmon and a cucumber slice. Top with bread slices or leave open-face; trim crusts and cut sandwiches into triangles. Arrange on a pretty plate and garnish with lemon wedges. Serve immediately or bread will become soggy.

Breads & Buns

Almost every region and town in England has its own version of a tea bread or bun. They are all slightly different, and all wonderfully tasty. Often served in place of more delicate sandwiches during winter, they're terrific for high tea.

If you're on a yeast-free diet or don't have much time, try making Crumpets, Baking Powder Tea Cakes or one of the other quick breads in this chapter.

Crumpets

3 cups all-purpose flour
1 (1/4-oz.) package active dry
   yeast
1-1/2 cups warm water
   (110F, 45C)
1/2 teaspoon baking soda
1 teaspoon salt
1 cup milk
Metal rings (see recipe
   introduction)
Butter
Jam

Crumpets are probably one of the most common English afternoon tea breads. Smooth and golden on one side, the other side is full of little holes through which the butter and jam drip!

Due to the rather thin consistency of the batter, crumpets need to be cooked in metal rings. Either poached egg or English muffin rings work fine, but if you don't happen to have such rings, improvise by cutting both the tops and bottoms from 6-1/2-ounce fish cans. Thoroughly wash and lightly grease the rings before heating them on the griddle or in the skillet. After the crumpets have cooked 3 to 4 minutes and the tops are quite holey and "set," the rings can be carefully removed, cooled and regreased for another batch. To hasten the cooking, you may also wish to use two skillets.

In a large bowl, combine flour and yeast. Add water and mix well. Cover with plastic wrap and let stand in a warm place for 1 hour or until batter has doubled in bulk and is puffy. Dissolve baking soda and salt in milk and add to batter. Stir vigorously until well mixed and batter is runny (beating helps to form the holes). Preheat a griddle or heavy skillet over medium heat. Grease very lightly; also grease metal rings and set on griddle to warm up. Pour about 2 tablespoons batter into each ring. Reduce heat to low and cook gently about 7 minutes or until underside is browned and top is covered with bubbles. Carefully remove rings. Turn and cook crumpets 2 to 3 minutes or just until lightly browned. Grease rings again and repeat with another batch. Cool crumpets completely. To serve, reheat by toasting both sides under a broiler. Serve warm with butter and jam. Makes about 25 crumpets.

Irish Soda Bread

4 cups all-purpose flour
1 teaspoon salt
1 teaspoon baking soda
2 tablespoons solid vegetable
   shortening, chilled, cut in
   chunks
1 cup buttermilk
Butter
Preserves

This yeast-free tea bread comes from the Emerald Isle.

Preheat oven to 400F (205C). Dust a medium-size baking sheet with flour; set aside. Sift 4 cups flour, salt and baking soda into a large bowl. With your fingers, rub in shortening until mixture is crumbly. Make a well in center of flour mixture. Add buttermilk and mix to form a soft dough. Turn out onto a lightly floured surface and knead very lightly. With your hands, form dough in a round about 2 inches thick. Place on baking sheet and score top in 4 straight lines with a sharp knife. Bake about 35 minutes or until bread is risen and bottom is browned. Transfer to a wire rack to cool. Serve warm with butter and preserves. Makes about 10 servings.

On the preceding pages: Pack a picnic hamper, grab a comfortable quilt to use as a cloth, and tote afternoon tea to a park or the garden. Oven Scones, page 67, Sausage Rolls, page 45, and Glazed Tea Ring, page 58, make up this pretty, and potable, display.

Baking Powder Tea Cakes

3 cups all-purpose flour
1-1/2 teaspoons baking
  powder
1/2 teaspoon salt
6 tablespoons cold butter,
  cut in small pieces
1/4 cup sugar
1/2 cup raisins
1 egg, beaten
Milk
Glaze (recipe follows)
Butter
Jam, if desired

Glaze:
1 tablespoon milk
2 teaspoons sugar

These quick, easy cakes are a real treat. Serve them fresh, lavished with butter (and jam, if you like).

Preheat oven to 425F (220C). Grease and lightly flour a large baking sheet; set aside. Sift flour, baking powder and salt into a large bowl. With your fingers, rub in 6 tablespoons butter until mixture is crumbly. Stir in sugar and raisins. Beat in egg and a little milk, a tablespoon at a time, to form a soft dough. Turn out onto a floured surface and knead briefly. Divide into 6 equal portions. With your hands, form dough in round, 1/2-inch-thick cakes. Place on baking sheet. Bake about 20 minutes or until light golden brown. Transfer to a wire rack. Prepare Glaze; brush over hot tea cakes. Cool briefly. Split and spread with butter. Serve with jam, if desired. Makes 6 tea cakes.

Glaze:
Stir together milk and sugar in a small cup until smooth.

Pikelets

1 cup self-rising flour
Pinch of salt
1/4 teaspoon baking soda
3 tablespoons sugar
1/2 cup sour milk
1 egg, lightly beaten
1 tablespoon butter, melted,
  cooled
Butter

These tea pancakes are easy to whip up in a hurry. If you don't happen to have sour milk on hand, simply stir 1 teaspoon of white vinegar or lemon juice into 1/2 cup of fresh milk and let it stand about 5 minutes before proceeding.

Preheat a griddle or heavy skillet over medium heat; grease lightly. Sift flour, salt and baking soda into a medium-size bowl. Stir in sugar. Stir in sour milk, egg and melted butter; mix well. Drop heaping tablespoonfuls of batter onto griddle. Cook about 2 minutes or until bottoms of pancakes are brown and bubbles form on top; flip over with a wide spatula and cook about 2 minutes longer or until browned on other side. Serve warm with butter. Makes about 10 pikelets.

Variation
Fruit Pikelets: Add 2 tablespoons raisins to batter.

Barm Bread

2 cups diced mixed dried
   fruit
1 cup plus 2 tablespoons
   packed brown sugar
2 cups cold, strong black tea
2-1/2 cups self-rising flour
1 egg, lightly beaten
Butter

This hearty, traditional bread from the north of England is delicious for a winter tea.

The night before baking, put dried fruit in a large bowl. Sprinkle with brown sugar. Add tea. Cover and let soak overnight. To bake bread, preheat oven to 350F (175C). Generously grease a 9" x 5" loaf pan. Sift flour into a medium-size bowl. Mix egg into dried fruit. Stir in flour just until well blended. Spoon into loaf pan; smooth top. Bake for 1-1/2 hours or until a wooden pick inserted in center comes out clean. Cool in pan 5 minutes, then turn out onto a wire rack. Serve warm or cold, cut in slices and spread with butter. Makes 8 to 10 servings.

English Muffins

4 cups all-purpose flour
1 (1/4-oz.) package active dry
   yeast
1 teaspoon superfine sugar
6 tablespoons warm water
   (110F, 45C)
1 teaspoon salt
2/3 cup lukewarm milk
2 tablespoons butter, melted,
   cooled
1 egg, lightly beaten
White cornmeal
Butter
Jam or honey, if desired

Though English muffins are eaten for breakfast in the United States, they're teatime fare in England. Especially good eaten around a blazing fire in the wintertime, muffins should be served drenched with melting butter and topped with jam or honey.

In a large bowl, combine 1/2 cup flour, yeast and superfine sugar. Add water and mix well. Let stand in a warm place about 20 minutes or until mixture is bubbly. Sift remaining 3-1/2 cups flour and salt into another large bowl. Stir milk, melted butter and egg into yeast mixture. Fold in dry ingredients and mix to form a soft dough. Turn out onto a lightly floured surface and knead about 10 minutes or until smooth and elastic. Place dough in a greased bowl; turn over to grease top. Cover and let rise in a warm place about 1-1/2 hours or until doubled in bulk. Grease and lightly flour a large baking sheet; set aside. Punch down dough; turn out onto floured surface and knead briefly to release air. Roll out about 1/2 inch thick with a floured rolling pin. Cut dough into 12 rounds with a 3-1/2-inch cookie cutter. Place rounds on baking sheet and lightly sprinkle with cornmeal. Cover and let rise in a warm place about 45 minutes or until doubled in bulk. Preheat oven to 450F (230C). Bake muffins 5 minutes, then turn over and bake 5 minutes longer or until light brown. Transfer to a wire rack to cool. To serve, toast lightly. Split and spread with butter. Serve with jam or honey, if desired. Makes 12 muffins.

Lightly toasted English Muffins, served with butter curls and a pot of homemade Raspberry Jam, page 156, are teatime favorites.

A fresh lemon juice-and-powdered sugar icing and a topping of chopped nuts finish off delightfully yeasty Glazed Tea Ring.

Glazed Tea Ring

2 cups all-purpose flour
1 (1/4-oz.) package active dry yeast
1 teaspoon superfine sugar
1/2 cup plus 2 tablespoons warm milk (110F, 45C)
1/2 teaspoon salt
1/4 cup granulated sugar
2 tablespoons butter, melted, cooled
1 egg, lightly beaten
Lemon Glaze (recipe follows)
2 tablespoons chopped nuts
Butter

This handsome braided bread has a tender, cakelike texture. A lemony glaze and a sprinkling of nuts make it pastry-shop pretty.

In a large bowl, combine 1/2 cup flour, yeast and superfine sugar. Add milk and mix well. Let stand in a warm place about 20 minutes or until mixture is bubbly. Sift remaining 1-1/2 cups flour and salt into a medium-size bowl. Stir in granulated sugar. Stir melted butter and egg into yeast mixture. Fold in dry ingredients and mix to form a soft dough. Turn out onto a lightly floured surface and knead about 10 minutes or until smooth and elastic. Place in a greased bowl; turn over to grease top. Cover and let rise in a warm place about 1-1/2 hours or until doubled in bulk. Grease a medium-size baking sheet; set aside. Punch down dough; turn out onto floured surface and knead briefly to release air. Divide dough in thirds; roll each piece with your hands to

Lemon Glaze:
1 cup powdered sugar
1-1/2 tablespoons lemon juice

make a rope about 18 inches long. Lightly press ropes together at 1 end. Place on baking sheet and braid loosely. Form into a ring and press ends together to seal. Cover and let rise in a warm place 15 minutes. Preheat oven to 450F (230C). Bake 25 minutes or until golden brown. Transfer to a wire rack to cool. When cooled, prepare glaze. Cover top of ring with glaze and sprinkle with nuts. Cut in slices and serve with butter. Makes about 10 servings.

Lemon Glaze:
Mix powdered sugar and lemon juice in a small bowl until smooth.

Lardy Cake

4 cups all-purpose flour
1 (1/4-oz.) package active dry yeast
1 teaspoon superfine sugar
1-1/4 cups warm water (110F, 45C)
2 teaspoons salt
1/2 cup shortening (see choices in recipe introduction), chilled, cut in small pieces
4 tablespoons sugar
1 teaspoon apple pie spice

Though called "cake," this is really a bread. It's another traditional recipe that's much tastier than the name implies! For the shortening, you can use lard (as in the original version), firm solid vegetable shortening or butter. A mixture of half lard or vegetable shortening and half butter actually produces the best texture and flavor.

In a large bowl, combine 1/2 cup flour, yeast and superfine sugar. Add water and mix well. Let stand in a warm place about 20 minutes or until mixture is frothy. Sift remaining 3-1/2 cups flour and salt into another large bowl. Make a well in center of flour mixture; add yeast mixture and stir to form a soft dough. Turn out onto a lightly floured surface and knead about 10 minutes or until smooth and elastic. Place dough in a lightly greased bowl; turn over to grease top. Cover and let rise in a warm place about 1-1/2 hours or until doubled in bulk. Grease a medium-size baking sheet; set aside. Punch down dough; turn out onto floured surface and knead briefly to release air. Roll into a 1/4-inch-thick rectangle with a floured rolling pin. Cover 2/3 of dough with 1/2 of shortening. Sprinkle 2 tablespoons granulated sugar and 1/2 teaspoon apple pie spice over shortening. Fold uncovered third of dough over shortening; then carefully fold over 1 more time to cover shortening completely. Roll out dough to a rectangle again. Cover 2/3 of dough with remaining 1/2 of shortening and sprinkle with remaining 2 tablespoons granulated sugar and 1/2 teaspoon apple pie spice. Fold and roll as before. With your hands, shape dough in an oval about 1/2 inch thick. Place on baking sheet. Cover and let rise in a warm place 30 minutes or until puffy. Preheat oven to 425F (220C). Bake about 30 minutes or until light golden brown. Serve warm, cut in slices. Makes about 10 servings.

Chelsea Buns

2 cups all-purpose flour
2 (1/4-oz.) packages active
 dry yeast
1 teaspoon superfine sugar
2/3 cup warm milk (110F,
 45C)
1/2 teaspoon salt
1 tablespoon cold butter, cut
 in small pieces
1 egg, beaten
2 tablespoons butter, melted,
 cooled
3/4 cup mixed currants and
 raisins
2 tablespoons chopped
 mixed candied peel
1/4 cup packed brown sugar
Honey

These wonderful sticky buns, named for the Chelsea district of London, are a teatime favorite all over England.

In a large bowl, combine 1/2 cup flour, yeast and superfine sugar. Add milk and mix well. Let stand in a warm place about 20 minutes or until mixture is bubbly. Sift remaining 1-1/2 cups flour and salt into a medium-size bowl. With your fingers, rub in cold butter until mixture is crumbly. Stir flour mixture and egg into yeast mixture. Beat to form a soft dough that cleans sides of bowl. Turn out onto a lightly floured surface and knead about 5 minutes or until smooth. Place in a greased bowl; turn over to grease top. Cover and let rise in a warm place about 45 minutes or until doubled in bulk. Grease a medium-size baking sheet; set aside. Punch down dough; turn out onto floured surface and knead briefly to release air. Roll into a 14" x 9" rectangle with a floured rolling pin. Brush with melted butter. In a small bowl, mix currants, raisins, candied peel and brown sugar; sprinkle over dough. Roll up jelly-roll style, starting from a long side. Moisten edge with water and press to seal. Cut crosswise in 9 slices. Place slices cut-side down on baking sheet. Cover and let rise in a warm place about 30 minutes or until puffy. Preheat oven to 375F (190C). Bake about 30 minutes or until golden brown. While still warm, moisten a pastry brush with water, dip in honey and brush over buns. Serve warm. Makes 9 buns.

Warm from the oven and brushed lightly with honey, Chelsea Buns fairly brim over with raisins, currants and mixed candied peel.

Devonshire Splits

1 teaspoon superfine sugar
1-1/4 cups warm milk (110F, 45C)
1 (1/4-oz.) package active dry yeast
1/4 cup butter, melted, cooled
2 tablespoons granulated sugar
4 cups all-purpose flour
1 teaspoon salt

These light buns are eaten much like Oven Scones (page 67). Split them, spread with strawberry jam and top with Devonshire or whipped cream.

In a small bowl, dissolve superfine sugar in 1/2 of the milk. Sprinkle with yeast and let stand in a warm place 20 minutes or until frothy. In another small bowl, combine melted butter, granulated sugar and remaining milk. Sift flour and salt into a large bowl; make a well in center. Combine yeast and butter mixtures; pour into well and beat to form an elastic dough. Turn out onto a lightly floured surface and knead about 5 minutes or until smooth. Place in a greased bowl; turn over to grease top. Cover and let rise in a warm place about 1-1/2 hours or until doubled in bulk. Grease a large baking sheet; set aside. Punch down dough; turn out onto lightly floured surface and knead briefly to release air. Divide in 15 pieces. Lightly knead each piece and shape in a ball. Place balls 2 inches apart on baking sheet and flatten slightly with your hand. Cover and let rise in a warm place 20 minutes. Preheat oven to 425F (220C). Bake 15 to 20 minutes or until light golden brown. Transfer to a wire rack to cool. Makes 15 buns.

Bath Buns

4 cups all-purpose flour
1 (1/4-oz.) package active dry yeast
1 teaspoon superfine sugar
2/3 cup warm milk (110F, 45C)
1/4 cup warm water (110F, 45C)
1/2 teaspoon salt
1/4 cup granulated sugar
1/4 cup butter, melted, cooled
3 eggs
1-1/4 cups raisins
10 sugar cubes, coarsely crushed
Butter

These popular tea buns are from the delightful town of Bath, situated in the south of England.

In a large bowl, combine 1/2 cup flour, yeast and superfine sugar. Add milk and water; mix well. Let stand in a warm place about 20 minutes or until mixture is frothy. Sift remaining 3-1/2 cups flour and salt into another large bowl. Stir in granulated sugar. Beat melted butter and 2 eggs into yeast mixture. Fold in flour mixture and raisins; mix to form a very soft dough. Turn out onto a lightly floured surface and knead about 5 minutes or until smooth. Place in a greased bowl; turn over to grease top. Cover and let rise in a warm place about 1-1/2 hours or until doubled in bulk. Grease a large baking sheet. Beat dough well with a heavy spoon or heavy-duty electric mixer to release air. Drop dough by tablespoonfuls 2 inches apart onto greased baking sheet. Cover and let rise in a warm place about 30 minutes or until puffy. Preheat oven to 375F (190C). Beat remaining egg and brush over buns; sprinkle with crushed sugar. Bake about 15 minutes or until golden. Transfer to a wire rack to cool. Split and serve warm or cold with butter. Makes about 18 buns.

Syrup Buns

1 teaspoon superfine sugar
2/3 cup warm milk (110F, 45C)
1 (1/4-oz.) package active dry yeast
2 cups all-purpose flour
1/2 teaspoon salt
2 tablespoons cold butter, cut in small pieces
1 egg, lightly beaten
Syrup

Syrup:
1/4 cup butter
2/3 cup packed brown sugar
1 tablespoon light corn syrup

Every English child loves "sticky buns" for tea—and these are as sticky as you can get!

In a small bowl, dissolve superfine sugar in milk. Sprinkle with yeast and let stand in a warm place 20 minutes or until frothy. Sift flour and salt into a large bowl. With your fingers, rub in butter until mixture is crumbly. Make a well in center of flour mixture; add yeast mixture and egg and beat to form a soft dough that cleans sides of bowl. Turn out onto a lightly floured surface and knead about 5 minutes or until smooth. Place in a greased bowl; turn over to grease top. Cover and let rise in a warm place about 1-1/2 hours or until doubled in bulk. Meanwhile, prepare Syrup. Grease an 8-inch-square baking pan; pour 1/2 of Syrup into pan. Punch down dough; turn out onto floured surface and knead briefly to release air. Roll into a 14" x 9" rectangle with a floured rolling pin. Spread dough with remaining Syrup. Roll up jelly-roll style, starting from a long side. Moisten edge with water and press to seal. Cut roll crosswise into 9 slices. Place slices cut-side down in pan. Cover and let rise in a warm place about 30 minutes or until puffy. Preheat oven to 400F (205C). Bake buns 25 to 30 minutes or until golden brown. Cool in pan on a wire rack 10 minutes. Turn out onto a serving plate; scrape any syrup from pan over buns. Serve warm. Makes 9 buns.

Syrup:
In a small saucepan, combine butter, brown sugar and corn syrup. Stir over low heat until sugar is dissolved.

Scones

The scone in all its delightful varieties is a cornerstone of afternoon tea: whatever else you serve, be sure to have scones! Scones should be eaten very fresh as they don't keep well. But, happily, they're so quick to make you can easily bake them while you prepare the rest of the tea.

Controversy rages in England about the proper pronunciation of the word "scone." Northerners and the Scots pronounce it as it is spelled—with a long "o" (as in "throne"). Southerners, however, pronounce it to rhyme with "gone"—and as the word derives from the Gaelic *sgonn*, meaning "big mouthful," it pains me to admit that the Southerners are probably right. But, however you say it, there isn't a more delicious mouthful imaginable!

Though "scones" and "teatime" are synonomous, there are many variations on the theme. Shapes, for example, can vary from fluted to round, or even free-form drop, depending upon the selection of cookie cutter or tablespoon and the consistency of the dough.

Fruit Scones

2-1/2 cups all-purpose flour
2 teaspoons baking powder
1 teaspoon baking soda
1/2 teaspoon salt
1/2 cup sugar
6 tablespoons cold butter,
** cut in small pieces**
1/2 cup raisins
1 egg, beaten
1/2 cup plain yogurt
Grated peel of 1/2 lemon
Milk for brushing on scones
Butter

These tangy delights are a little heavier than plain oven scones. Make them slightly smaller and serve without the jam and cream.

Preheat oven to 425F (220C). Lightly grease a large baking sheet; set aside. Sift flour, baking powder, baking soda and salt into a large bowl. Stir in sugar. With your fingers, rub in butter pieces until mixture is crumbly. Mix in raisins. With a fork, stir in egg, yogurt and lemon peel and blend well to make a dough that *barely* holds together (you may need to press dough together with your hands). Turn out onto a floured surface. Roll out with a floured rolling pin or pat dough with your hands to make a round about 1/2 inch thick. Cut in rounds with a 1-1/2-inch fluted or plain cookie cutter. Place 1 to 1-1/2 inches apart on baking sheet; brush tops lightly with milk. Bake 10 to 12 minutes or until scones are well risen and golden. Transfer to a wire rack to cool 5 minutes. Split and serve warm with butter. Makes about 18 scones.

On the preceding pages: Freshly baked Rich Oven Scones, page 67, await on the side table, ready to be served with Caviar Puffs, page 46, both fine choices for "power" tea, a relatively new type of tea theme which is described on page 20.

Oven Scones

2 cups self-rising flour
1 tablespoon baking powder
Pinch of salt
2 tablespoons cold butter,
   cut in small pieces
1 to 1-1/3 cups milk, plus a
   little for brushing on
   scones
Butter

This basic oven scone is what's used for the famous "cream tea." Serve the scones fresh and warm from the oven accompanied by a pot of jam—preferably strawberry—and a dish of cream. Ideally, the cream should be clotted cream, that particularly rich variety that comes from Devonshire in England. English cream is difficult to get in the United States, but a few specialty stores do import it so check your local gourmet emporia. Failing that, serve a dish of unsweetened whipped cream. To eat, split your scone, generously spread each piece with jam and top with a spoonful of cream.

Preheat oven to 450F (230C). Very lightly grease a large baking sheet; set aside. Sift flour, baking powder and salt into a large bowl. With your fingers, rub in butter until mixture is crumbly. Make a well in center of mixture; add milk and mix with a fork to make a dough that *barely* holds together (you may need to press dough together with your hands). Turn out onto a floured surface and knead lightly just until smooth. Roll out with a floured rolling pin or pat dough with your hands to make a round about 3/4 inch thick. Cut in rounds with a 2-inch fluted or plain cookie cutter. Arrange 1 to 1-1/2 inches apart on baking sheet; brush tops lightly with milk. Bake 8 to 10 minutes or until well risen and golden. Transfer to a wire rack and cool 5 minutes. Split and serve warm with butter. Makes about 12 scones.

Variation
Rich Oven Scones: Add 1 tablespoon sugar to the dry ingredients. In place of the 2/3 cup milk, use a mixture of 1 lightly beaten egg and 5 tablespoons milk.

Caribbean Scones

1 cup all-purpose flour
2 teaspoons baking powder
1/2 teaspoon salt
1 teaspoon sugar
1 cup mashed cooked sweet
   potatoes
3 tablespoons butter, melted,
   cooled
Butter
Honey, if desired

West Indians living in England have created this deliciously exotic adaptation of the good old scone.

Preheat oven to 375F (190C). Grease a baking sheet; set aside. Sift flour, baking powder and salt into a medium-size bowl; stir in sugar. In a large bowl, thoroughly mix potatoes and 1-1/2 tablespoons melted butter with a fork. Add dry ingredients and mix to form a soft dough. Turn out onto a floured surface. Roll out with a floured rolling pin or pat dough with your hands to make a round about 1/2 inch thick. Cut in rounds with a 2-inch fluted or plain cookie cutter. Place 1 to 1-1/2 inches apart on baking sheet; brush tops with remaining 1-1/2 tablespoons melted butter. Bake about 20 minutes or until light brown. Split and serve warm with butter and honey. Makes about 10 scones.

Welsh Batch Scone

2 cups self-rising flour
1/4 teaspoon ground
    cinnamon
1/4 teaspoon ground ginger
1/4 teaspoon ground cloves
1/4 teaspoon ground mace
1/4 teaspoon ground
    coriander
1/2 cup solid vegetable
    shortening, chilled, cut in
    chunks
3/4 cup superfine sugar
1/4 cup raisins
1/3 cup pitted dates,
    quartered
About 1/4 cup milk
1 egg yolk, beaten
1 tablespoon packed light
    brown sugar
Butter

This rich and spicy scone is baked in one big piece.

Preheat oven to 400F (205C). Grease a large baking sheet; set aside. Sift flour, cinnamon, ginger, cloves, mace and coriander into a large bowl. With your fingers, rub in shortening until mixture is crumbly. Add sugar, raisins and dates; mix well. Gradually add enough milk to form a lumpy dough, mixing with a fork. Turn out onto baking sheet and pat with your hands to make an 8-inch round about 3/4 inch thick. With a sharp knife, score top in 8 wedges. Brush with egg yolk and sprinkle with brown sugar. Bake about 20 minutes or until golden brown. Transfer scone to wire rack and cool about 5 minutes. Serve warm with butter. Makes 8 servings.

Cheese Scones

1 cup all-purpose flour
1-1/2 teaspoons baking
    powder
1 teaspoon dry mustard
Pinch of salt
1 cup whole-wheat flour
3 tablespoons cold butter or
    margarine, cut in small
    pieces
3/4 cup (3 oz.) finely
    shredded sharp Cheddar
    cheese
About 2/3 cup milk
Butter

Try these savory treats when you're in the mood for a scone that's a bit different from the usual.

Preheat oven to 425F (220C). Lightly grease a large baking sheet; set aside. Sift all-purpose flour, baking powder, dry mustard and salt into a large bowl. Stir in whole-wheat flour. With your fingers, rub in cold butter until mixture is crumbly. Stir in 1/2 cup cheese. Make a well in center of mixture; add milk and mix with a fork to make a dough that *barely* holds together (you may need to press dough together with your hands). Turn out onto a floured surface and knead lightly. Roll out with a floured rolling pin or pat dough with your hands to make a round about 3/4 inch thick. Cut in rounds with a 2-inch fluted or plain cookie cutter. Place 1 to 1-1/2 inches apart on baking sheet; sprinkle with remaining 1/4 cup cheese. Bake 8 to 10 minutes or until well risen and golden. Transfer to a wire rack to cool. When cold, split and serve with butter. Makes about 12 scones.

On the preceding pages: Sweet potatoes give character to the round Caribbean Scones, page 67; spicy raisin- and date-filled Welsh Batch Scone, above, is formed in a single round and cut into wedges before serving; and fluted Oven Scones, page 67, presented as for the famous English "cream tea," are generously spread with strawberry jam and topped with Devonshire cream.

Brown sugar and egg yolk give Welsh Batch Scone an attractive, deep-golden glaze. This favorite is baked in a single large round and cut into wedges while it is still warm, just before serving with butter and perhaps a touch of jam or preserves.

Whole-Wheat Banana Scones

1 cup self-rising flour
1/2 teaspoon salt
1 cup whole-wheat self-rising flour
2 tablespoons cold butter, cut in small pieces
About 1/2 cup milk, plus a little for brushing on scones
2 tablespoons honey
2 medium-size ripe bananas, mashed
Butter

These are a little heartier than traditional scones.

Preheat oven to 450F (230C). Lightly grease a large baking sheet. Sift self-rising flour and salt into a large bowl; stir in whole-wheat flour. With your fingers, rub in butter until mixture is crumbly. Make a well in center of mixture. Pour in 1/2 cup milk and the honey and mix well. Add bananas and mix with a fork to form a soft dough. Turn out onto a floured surface and knead lightly. Roll out with a floured rolling pin or pat dough with your hands to make a round about 3/4 inch thick. Cut in rounds with a 2-inch fluted or plain cookie cutter. Place 1 to 1-1/2 inches apart on baking sheet; brush tops lightly with milk. Bake 10 to 12 minutes or until well risen and browned on bottom. Transfer to a wire rack and cool 5 minutes. Split and serve warm with butter. Makes about 16 scones.

Spud Scones

1 pound potatoes
2 teaspoons salt
3 tablespoons butter, room
   temperature
About 1 cup (4-oz.)
   self-rising flour
Butter

These unusual potato scones offer an ideal way to use up leftover boiled or mashed potatoes. You can also use instant mashed potato mix, but the result will be much fresher, lighter scones if you cook the potatoes especially for them.

Partially fill a large saucepan with cold water. Peel potatoes; cut in quarters and add to pan. Bring to a boil, then reduce heat, cover and simmer briskly about 15 minutes or until potatoes are tender. Drain well; place in a large bowl and mash coarsely with a potato masher or fork. Add salt and 3 tablespoons butter and continue to mash until potatoes are smooth. Mix in enough flour, 1 tablespoon at a time, to form a stiff dough. Preheat griddle or heavy skillet over high heat; grease lightly. Turn dough onto a floured surface and knead lightly. Roll out with a floured rolling pin to a thickness of 1/4 inch. Cut in rounds with a 2-inch fluted or plain cookie cutter. Cook on griddle or skillet 4 to 5 minutes on each side or until golden brown. Serve hot with butter. Makes 12 to 15 scones.

Treacle Scones

2 cups all-purpose flour
1-1/2 teaspoons baking
   powder
Pinch of salt
2-1/2 tablespoons light
   molasses
2 tablespoons butter
About 1/4 cup milk
Butter

In England, molasses is known as treacle. These fragrant, chewy scones are perfect for tea when there is a nip in the air.

Preheat oven to 400F (205C). Lightly grease a large baking sheet; set aside. Sift flour, baking powder and salt into a large bowl; set aside. In a medium-size saucepan, combine molasses and 2 tablespoons butter; stir over low heat until butter is melted. Make a well in center of dry ingredients; add molasses mixture and milk and mix with a fork to form a soft dough. Turn out onto a floured surface. Roll out with a floured rolling pin or pat dough with your hands to make a round about 1/2 inch thick. Cut in rounds with a 2-inch fluted or plain cookie cutter. Place 1 to 1-1/2 inches apart on baking sheet. Bake 10 to 12 minutes or until well risen and golden. Transfer to a wire rack and cool 5 minutes. Split and serve warm with butter. Makes 12 to 15 scones.

Drop Scones have an almost crumpet-like look about them, though the texture more closely resembles a pancake.

Drop Scones

1 cup all-purpose flour
Pinch of baking soda
Pinch of salt
3 tablespoons sugar
2/3 cup buttermilk
1 egg, lightly beaten
2 teaspoons butter, melted,
  cooled
Butter

This version of the scone originates in Scotland. It's sometimes known as "Scots pancake," which seems like a more accurate name!

Preheat a griddle or heavy skillet over high heat; grease lightly. Sift flour, baking soda and salt into a large bowl. Stir in sugar. Add buttermilk, egg and melted butter and mix well with a wooden spoon. Drop tablespoonfuls of batter onto griddle or skillet, spacing scones well apart. Cook a few minutes or until tops are bubbling and undersides are golden brown; flip over with a wide spatula and cook until brown on other side. As scones are cooked, wrap them in a cloth towel or napkin to keep them moist and warm while you cook remaining scones. Serve warm with butter. Makes 12 to 15 scones.

Variation
Fruit Drop Scones: Add 1/2 cup raisins to dry ingredients.

Cookies

In England, tea and biscuits is as ubiquitous a combination as milk and cookies on this side of the Atlantic. But English "biscuits" are the same as American cookies—and to complicate matters further, what Americans call biscuits are more like English scones (see pages 64-73)! To avoid any confusion, I've called the recipes in this chapter "cookies" but, by any name, they're an essential component of afternoon tea. Typically, tea cookies are small and quite rich. This collection of recipes is a particularly sophisticated selection. If you can, make them the day you are entertaining: it's wonderful when the aroma of freshly baked cookies greets guests as they arrive at your home.

Shrewsbury Cookies

2 cups all-purpose flour
Grated peel of 1 lemon
1/2 cup butter or margarine,
    room temperature
1/2 cup superfine sugar
1 egg yolk

Crisp and light, these cookies just melt in your mouth.

Preheat oven to 350F (175C). Grease a large baking sheet; set aside. Sift flour into a medium-size bowl; stir in lemon peel. Set aside. In a large bowl, cream butter and superfine sugar with an electric mixer or a wooden spoon until light and fluffy. Add egg yolk and beat well. With wooden spoon, gradually work in flour mixture to make a firm dough. Turn out onto a lightly floured surface. With a floured rolling pin, roll out to a thickness of 1/8 inch. Cut in rounds with a 2-1/2-inch plain or fluted cookie cutter. Place on baking sheet and bake about 15 minutes or until light brown. Transfer to a wire rack and cool completely. Makes about 24 cookies.

Whole-Wheat Digestives

1 cup all-purpose flour
1/2 teaspoon salt
2 cups whole-wheat flour
6 tablespoons cold
    margarine, cut in small
    pieces
1/4 cup solid vegetable
    shortening, chilled, cut in
    chunks
1/2 cup packed light brown
    sugar
1 egg
1/4 cup water

Digestive biscuits are a little like American graham crackers. They're probably the most common of all English tea cookies, often eaten in offices and factories with afternoon tea. Though excellent commercial brands are available, home-baked digestives are doubly delicious—and great for dunking!

Preheat oven to 350F (175C). Grease 2 large baking sheets; set aside. Sift all-purpose flour and salt into a large bowl; stir in whole-wheat flour. With your fingers, rub in margarine and shortening until mixture is crumbly. Stir in brown sugar. Beat together egg and water; add to flour mixture and stir with a wooden spoon to form a soft dough. Turn onto a lightly floured surface. With a floured rolling pin, roll out about 1/8 inch thick. Cut in rounds with a 2-inch cookie cutter and place on baking sheets. Prick tops with a fork. Bake about 15 minutes or until cookies are light brown. Carefully transfer to a wire rack to cool. Makes about 50 cookies.

Variation
Chocolate Digestives: Coat backs of cooled cookies with melted semi-sweet chocolate. For a full batch of digestives, you'll need 6 to 8 ounces of chocolate.

On the preceding pages: A formal tea buffet includes a tempting array of savories and sweets. Counterclockwise, from the left foreground: Strawberry-topped Victoria Sandwich Sponge, page 106; assorted tea sandwiches, pages 48-51; Pâté Rounds, page 42, arranged alternately with Savory Tartlets, page 40; Featherweight Chocolate Chip Cookies, page 146; Scotch Oatmeal Cookies, page 80; and Orange Tea Loaf, page 116, elegantly displayed on doily-topped trays and platters.

Chocolate Raspberry Rings

1-3/4 cups all-purpose flour
1/4 cup unsweetened cocoa
   powder
1/2 cup butter or margarine,
   room temperature
1/2 cup superfine sugar
1 egg yolk
Glacé Icing (recipe follows)
About 1/2 cup raspberry jam

Glacé Icing:
3/4 cup powdered sugar
1 to 2 tablespoons warm
   water

Arranged on a doily, these cookies make a particularly pretty presentation.

Preheat oven to 350F (175C). Grease 2 large baking sheets; set aside. Sift flour and cocoa into a medium-size bowl; set aside. In a large bowl, cream butter and superfine sugar with an electric mixer or a wooden spoon until light and fluffy. Add egg yolk and beat well. With wooden spoon, gradually work in dry ingredients to make a firm dough. Turn out onto a lightly floured surface. With a floured rolling pin, roll out to a thickness of 1/8 inch. Cut in rounds with a 2-1/2-inch plain or fluted cookie cutter. Cut out centers of half the cookies with a round 1-inch cookie cutter; re-roll centers to make more cookies. Place rounds and rings on baking sheets and bake about 15 minutes or until set and browned on bottoms. Transfer cookies to a wire rack and cool completely. Prepare Glacé Icing. Spread icing over rings. Cover solid rounds with jam. Place rings atop rounds so jam shows through center. Makes about 15 cookies.

Glacé Icing:
Sift powdered sugar into a small bowl. Gradually add water and stir until smooth. Icing should be thick enough to coat the back of a spoon.

Cornish Fairings

1-1/4 cups self-rising flour
2/3 cup semolina flour
1/4 teaspoon ground
   cinnamon
1/4 teaspoon ground ginger
1/2 cup sugar
1/2 cup cold butter, cut in
   small pieces
1 egg, beaten

Another of those oddly named English recipes! This one's for a ginger cookie.

Preheat oven to 350F (175C). Grease 2 large baking sheets; set aside. Sift flours, cinnamon and ginger into a large bowl. Stir in sugar. With your fingers, rub butter into dry ingredients until mixture is crumbly. Work in egg. Knead dough in bowl until smooth. Turn out onto a lightly floured surface. With a floured rolling pin, roll out to a thickness of 1/8 inch. Cut into rounds with a 2-inch cookie cutter and place on baking sheets. Bake about 15 minutes or until golden brown. Transfer to a wire rack to cool. Makes about 24 cookies.

Chocolate Chip Dainties

1 cup all-purpose flour
1/2 teaspoon baking soda
1/2 teaspoon cream of tartar
Pinch of salt
1/2 cup butter, room
    temperature
1/2 cup packed light brown
    sugar
1 egg
1/2 teaspoon vanilla extract
1/4 cup chopped walnuts
1/2 (6-oz.) package (1/2 cup)
    semisweet chocolate pieces

These are lighter than the usual type of chocolate chip cookie.

Sift flour, baking soda, cream of tartar and salt into a medium-size bowl; set aside. In a large bowl, cream butter and brown sugar with an electric mixer or a wooden spoon until light and fluffy. Add egg and beat well. Beat in vanilla. With wooden spoon, gradually work in dry ingredients until well blended. Stir in walnuts and chocolate pieces. Chill dough until firm. Preheat oven to 350F (175C). Grease 2 large baking sheets. With your fingers, pinch off pieces of dough and roll into walnut-size balls. Place about 2 inches apart on baking sheets. Bake 12 to 15 minutes or until light brown. Transfer to a wire rack to cool. Makes about 30 cookies.

Brandy Snaps

1/2 cup all-purpose flour
1/2 teaspoon ground ginger
6 tablespoons butter
1/4 cup superfine sugar
1/4 cup light corn syrup
1 teaspoon brandy
Grated peel of 1/2 lemon

Light and lacy, these are sophisticated teatime treats.

Preheat oven to 350F (175C). Cover as many baking sheets as you have (3 to 4 will be helpful) with parchment paper. Grease handles of several wooden spoons. Sift flour and ginger into a small bowl; set aside. In a medium-size saucepan, heat butter, superfine sugar and corn syrup over low heat until butter is melted and sugar is dissolved. Remove from heat. Add flour mixture and stir until smooth. Stir in brandy and lemon peel. Drop teaspoonfuls of batter about 4 inches apart on baking sheets. Bake cookies, 1 sheet at a time, 7 to 10 minutes or until golden. Cool on baking sheets 1 to 2 minutes but do not allow to harden. Remove cookies with a wide spatula and roll each around a wooden spoon handle. Cool completely, then gently twist off. Makes about 20 cookies.

Variation
Pipe whipped cream into centers of snaps before serving.

Buttery rich and delicately flavored, Classic Shortbread is appropriate on any afternoon tea menu.

Classic Shortbread

2 cups all-purpose flour
1 cup cornstarch
Pinch of salt
1 cup butter, room
   temperature
1 cup superfine sugar
1 tablespoon granulated
   sugar

These ultra-rich cookies are a luxurious teatime favorite.

Preheat oven to 325F (165C). Sift flour, cornstarch and salt into a medium-size bowl; set aside. In a large bowl, cream butter and superfine sugar with an electric mixer or a wooden spoon until light and fluffy. With wooden spoon, gradually work in dry ingredients until thoroughly mixed. Press dough into an ungreased shallow 11" x 7" or 9" square baking pan. Prick surface all over with a fork. With a knife, lightly score surface in 20 squares about 1-1/2" x 2". Bake about 40 minutes or until light golden. Sprinkle with granulated sugar. Cool in pan. To serve, cut into marked squares with a sharp knife. Makes about 20 cookies.

Scotch Oatmeal Cookies

1 cup all-purpose flour
1/2 teaspoon baking soda
1 teaspoon salt
3/4 cup butter, room temperature
1 cup packed dark brown sugar
1/2 cup granulated sugar
1 egg
1/2 cup plain yogurt
1 teaspoon Scotch whisky
2 cups regular rolled oats

Technically, the correct terms to describe something or someone from Scotland are "Scottish" and "Scots." "Scotch" used to only refer to whisky made in Scotland, but it has become more commonly used—as you will note in "Scotch eggs." In this instance, the word is used correctly!

Preheat oven to 350F (175C). Grease 2 large baking sheets; set aside. Sift flour, baking soda and salt into a medium-size bowl; set aside. In a large bowl, cream butter and sugars with an electric mixer or a wooden spoon until light and fluffy. Add egg, yogurt and whisky and beat well. With wooden spoon, gradually work in dry ingredients until well blended. Stir in rolled oats. Drop teaspoonfuls of dough about 2 inches apart on baking sheets. Bake about 12 minutes or until golden on top and browned around edges. Transfer to a wire rack to cool. Makes about 40 cookies.

Almond Slices

2 cups all-purpose flour
Pinch of salt
6 tablespoons cold butter or margarine, cut in small pieces
1-1/4 cups sugar
2 eggs, separated
About 1/3 cup apricot jam
1 cup ground almonds
2 drops almond extract

Butter-cookie base, jam filling, almond meringue topping—the combination of textures makes these rich "biscuits" extra-delicious.

Preheat oven to 375F (190C). Grease a 13" x 9" baking pan; set aside. Sift flour and salt into a large bowl. With your fingers, rub in butter until mixture is crumbly. Add 1/4 cup of the sugar. Stir in egg yolks to form a stiff dough. Turn dough into pan and press to form an even layer. Spread dough with jam (if jam is too stiff to spread, warm it over low heat). In a medium-size bowl, beat egg whites until stiff peaks form. Gradually beat in remaining 1 cup sugar. Fold in almonds and almond extract. Spread meringue over jam. Bake about 25 minutes or until topping is set and light brown. Cool in pan. To serve, cut in slices. Makes about 24 slices.

It's difficult to discern exactly what gives the subtle flavor nuance to Scotch Oatmeal Cookies. Surprise! It's a touch of Scotch whisky.

Jumbals

1-1/2 cups all-purpose flour
Grated peel of 1 lemon
1/2 cup butter, room
   temperature
1/2 cup superfine sugar
1 egg yolk
1/2 cup ground almonds

Also called "jumbles," these oddly named cookies reputedly date back to the War of the Roses in the 1400s.

Preheat oven to 350F (175C). Grease 2 large baking sheets; set aside. Sift flour into a medium-size bowl; stir in lemon peel. Set aside. In a large bowl, cream butter and superfine sugar with an electric mixer or a wooden spoon until light and fluffy. Add egg yolk and beat well. With wooden spoon, gradually work in flour mixture. Stir in almonds. Turn out onto a lightly floured surface. With a floured rolling pin, roll out to a thickness of 1/8 inch. Cut into strips 1/2-inch-wide and 4-inches long. Arrange strips on baking sheets, curving each into an "S" shape. Bake about 15 minutes or until pale golden. Transfer to a wire rack to cool. Makes about 20 cookies.

Coconut Mounds

2 egg whites, room
   temperature
1/4 teaspoon salt
1/4 cup sugar
1/2 teaspoon almond extract
1/2 cup sweetened flaked
   coconut

In some areas these cookies are called macaroons.

Preheat oven to 250F (120C). Grease a large baking sheet; set aside. In a medium-size bowl, beat egg whites with salt until soft peaks form. Gradually add sugar, beating constantly until stiff but not dry. Gently but thoroughly fold in almond extract and coconut. Place tablespoonfuls of mixture on baking sheet. Bake 40 minutes. Turn off heat but leave cookies in oven about 1-1/2 hours or until oven has cooled completely. Makes about 18 cookies.

Macaroons

1/2 cup ground almonds
2/3 cup superfine sugar
1/2 teaspoon almond extract
1 egg white, room
   temperature
About 10 slivered almonds
Egg white for glaze

Some macaroon recipes contain coconut, but this version has only almonds. If you like coconut, try the preceding recipe for Coconut Mounds.

Preheat oven to 350F (175C). Cover a large baking sheet with parchment paper; set aside. In a medium-size bowl, mix ground almonds and superfine sugar. Stir in almond extract. In another medium-size bowl, beat 1 egg white until it holds stiff peaks. Fold in almond mixture. Place heaping teaspoonfuls of mixture 2 inches apart on baking sheet. Top each with a slivered almond. Lightly beat remaining egg white. Using a pastry brush, glaze each macaroon with egg white. Bake about 20 minutes or until macaroons are just turning a toasty brown. Transfer to a wire rack to cool. Makes about 10 cookies.

Cranberry Oatmeal Cookies are practically a requirement of wintertime tea. The bright berries provide a momentary burst of tartness as one bites into the chewy morsels, which are liberally spiced with cinnamon and nutmeg.

Cranberry Oatmeal Cookies

1-1/2 cups all-purpose flour
1 teaspoon baking soda
1 teaspoon baking powder
1 teaspoon salt
1-1/2 teaspoons ground
cinnamon
1/4 teaspoon ground nutmeg
1 cup butter or margarine,
room temperature
1-1/2 cups packed dark
brown sugar
2 eggs
1/2 cup buttermilk
3 cups quick-cooking rolled
oats
1-1/2 cups cranberries,
coarsely chopped

You can substitute frozen cranberries for fresh, but be sure to thaw them first.

Preheat oven to 400F (205C). Grease 2 or 3 large baking sheets; set aside. Sift flour, baking soda, baking powder, salt, cinnamon and nutmeg into a medium-size bowl; set aside. In a large bowl, cream butter and brown sugar with an electric mixer or a wooden spoon until fluffy. Beat in eggs 1 at a time. Stir in buttermilk. Add dry ingredients and mix well. Stir in rolled oats and cranberries. Drop tablespoonfuls of dough 2 inches apart on baking sheets. Bake about 10 minutes or until cookies are browned around edges. Transfer to a wire rack to cool. Makes about 60 cookies.

Pies & Pastries

Pastry-making is a very old craft indeed. It has its roots in Norman England, when meat was first encased in a water-and-flour paste to prevent it from drying out during cooking.

Pastries as we know them—made with various types of fat and more refined techniques—developed during the Middle Ages and reached a peak of popularity during Victorian times, when many of the delicious recipes that follow were developed. Sweet and savory pies have continued to be an integral part of every English cook's repertoire, and many a reputation has been made, or broken, on the tenderness of a tart shell.

Short-Crust Pastry

2 cups all-purpose flour
Pinch of salt
1/2 cup cold butter, cut in
  small pieces
1/2 cup solid vegetable
  shortening, chilled, cut in
  pieces
3 to 4 tablespoons cold water

Quick and easy to make, this basic pastry is suitable for both sweet and savory dishes. To insure tender, flaky pastry, keep the dough as cool as possible while preparing. Chill the bowl, the knives or pastry blender and even the rolling surface, and handle the dough as little as possible to avoid warming it with your hands.

Sift flour and salt into a medium-size bowl. With 2 knives or a pastry blender, cut in butter and shortening until mixture is crumbly. Gradually sprinkle in water, mixing with a knife until dough comes away cleanly from sides of bowl. Turn out onto a lightly floured surface and knead very lightly just until dough holds together. Wrap in parchment paper or waxed paper and refrigerate 30 minutes before using. Makes 2 cups pastry.

Rich Short-Crust Pastry

2 cups all-purpose flour
Pinch of salt
1 tablespoon superfine sugar
1/2 cup cold butter, cut in
  small pieces
1 egg yolk
2 teaspoons lemon juice
About 1 tablespoon cold
  water, if needed

Egg yolk enriches this pastry. If you're using it for a savory pie or tart, omit the sugar. Note that all short-crust pastries can be sealed airtight in a plastic bag and stored in the refrigerator several days or in the freezer up to 1 month (thaw before using).

Sift flour and salt into a medium-size bowl. Stir in superfine sugar. With 2 knives or a pastry blender, cut in butter until mixture is crumbly. In a small bowl, stir together egg yolk and lemon juice. Add to flour mixture and mix with a knife until dough comes away cleanly from sides of bowl; if necessary, add water to give dough correct consistency. Turn out onto a lightly floured surface and knead very lightly just until dough holds together. Wrap in parchment paper or waxed paper and refrigerate 30 minutes before using. Makes 2 cups pastry.

On the preceding pages: A baby shower tea is a delightful occasion in itself, but even more so when you bring forth Chocolate Mousse, page 131, Pastry Windmills, page 99, and Drop Scones, page 73, to be served with Lemon Curd, page 155.

Pie weights, uncooked beans or rice used in "blind baking" assure pastry crusts stay put and keep shrinkage to a minimum.

Sweet Short-Crust Pastry

2 cups all-purpose flour
Pinch of salt
2-1/2 teaspoons superfine
sugar
1 cup cold unsalted butter,
cut in small pieces
3 to 4 tablespoons cold water

The perfect choice for fruit-filled and other sweet tarts. Remember when rolling out pastry to flour both the rolling pin and the work surface very lightly. If you use too much flour, you'll roll flour into the dough and change its consistency.

Sift flour and salt into a medium-size bowl. Stir in superfine sugar. With 2 knives or a pastry blender, cut in butter until mixture is crumbly. Gradually sprinkle in water, mixing with a knife until dough comes away cleanly from sides of bowl. Turn out onto a lightly floured surface and knead very lightly just until dough holds together. Wrap in parchment paper or waxed paper and refrigerate 30 minutes before using. Makes 2 cups pastry.

Pâte Sucrée

2 cups all-purpose flour
1/2 cup powdered sugar
1/2 cup cold butter, cut in
    small pieces
2 egg yolks
Ice water, if needed

Ideal for small tarts and pastries, this basic French pastry holds its shape well when baked.

Sift flour and powdered sugar into a medium-size bowl. With 2 knives or a pastry blender, cut in butter until mixture is crumbly. Add egg yolks and mix with a knife until dough comes away cleanly from sides of bowl. If necessary, add a little water, a few drops at a time, to give dough correct consistency. Turn out onto a lightly floured surface and knead very lightly just until dough holds together. Wrap in parchment paper or waxed paper and refrigerate 1 hour before using. Makes 2 cups pastry.

Pâte Brisée

1-1/2 cups all-purpose flour
1/4 teaspoon salt
1/2 cup cold butter, cut in
    small pieces
3 to 5 tablespoons ice water

A high ratio of fat to flour gives this pastry its melt-in-the-mouth texture.

Sift flour and salt into a medium-size bowl. With 2 knives or a pastry blender, cut in butter until mixture is crumbly. Gradually sprinkle in 3 tablespoons ice water and mix with a knife until dough comes away cleanly from sides of bowl. If necessary, sprinkle in a little more water, mixing constantly. Turn out onto a lightly floured surface and knead very lightly just until dough holds together. Wrap in parchment paper or waxed paper and refrigerate 1 hour before using. Makes 1-1/2 cups pastry.

Though double-crust pies are generally too heavy for tea fare, single-crust pies and tarts are perfect. Tarts filled with fresh seasonal fruits taste luscious and look beautiful on your table, too. Meringue-topped pies are another wonderful choice, as are Bakewell Tart, Bonnie Doon Pie and the other delightful British specialties included in this chapter.

Pear & Walnut Tart

Walnut Topping (recipe follows)
1/2 recipe Sweet Short-Crust Pastry, page 87, or Pâte Sucrée, page 88
1 egg
2 tablespoons superfine sugar
1/2 teaspoon salt
1/4 teaspoon ground ginger
1/4 teaspoon ground nutmeg
1/4 teaspoon ground cinnamon
Grated peel of 1 lemon
1/2 pint (1 cup) dairy sour cream
3 medium-size ripe pears, peeled, halved lengthwise, cored

Walnut Topping:
2 tablespoons all-purpose flour, sifted
3 tablespoons packed light brown sugar
1/3 cup cold unsalted butter, cut in small pieces
1/4 teaspoon ground nutmeg
1/4 cup chopped walnuts

A little spicy, a lot fruity, this luscious tart is a wonderful way to celebrate the pear harvest.

⤷ Preheat oven to 400F (205C). Grease a 9-inch fluted tart pan with a removable bottom. Prepare Walnut Topping; set aside. On a lightly floured surface, thinly roll out pastry with a floured rolling pin. Line tart pan with pastry; lightly prick bottom of tart shell with a fork. Set aside. In a medium-size bowl, lightly beat egg. Thoroughly blend in superfine sugar, salt, ginger, nutmeg, cinnamon, lemon peel and sour cream. Arrange pears cut-side down in pastry shell with stem ends to center. Spoon sour cream mixture over pears. Sprinkle with Walnut Topping. Bake about 25 minutes or until pears are soft when pierced and a wooden pick inserted in filling comes out clean. Cool in pan on a wire rack. Remove pan sides before serving. Serve warm or cold. Makes 8 servings.

Walnut Topping:
Combine flour, brown sugar, butter and nutmeg in a blender or food processor and process until crumbly. Mix in walnuts. (Or place flour in a small bowl and rub in butter with your fingers until mixture is crumbly. Stir in brown sugar and nutmeg, then mix in walnuts.)

Bonnie Doon Pie

1 recipe Sweet Short-Crust
 Pastry, page 87
6 large tart apples, peeled,
 cored, sliced
1 tablespoon water
3/4 cup packed light brown
 sugar
Grated peel of 1/2 lemon
1/2 cup butter, room
 temperature
1/2 cup superfine sugar
2 eggs
1/4 cup all-purpose flour,
 sifted
1 cup ground almonds
1/4 teaspoon almond extract
Powdered sugar

As you might guess from the name, this pie is from Scotland. The flavor is better the day after baking so store the pie overnight in an airtight container before serving.

Preheat oven to 350F (175C). Grease a 9-inch springform pan. On a lightly floured surface, thinly roll out about 2/3 of pastry with a floured rolling pin. Line bottom and sides of pan with pastry; reserve pastry trimmings. Set pan aside. In a medium-size saucepan, combine apples, water, brown sugar and lemon peel. Cover and cook over medium heat, stirring often, until apples are soft. Remove from heat and beat well with a wooden spoon, or puree in a blender. Set aside to cool. In a medium-size bowl, cream butter and superfine sugar with an electric mixer or a wooden spoon until fluffy. Beat in eggs 1 at a time. Gently but thoroughly fold in flour, almonds and almond extract. Spread apple puree over bottom of pastry shell. Carefully spread almond mixture over puree. Combine remaining 1/3 of pastry and reserved pastry trimmings; roll out thinly, then cut in strips 1/2-inch-wide. Arrange strips in a lattice pattern over top of pie. Bake 30 to 40 minutes or until pastry is golden brown. Transfer to a wire rack to cool completely. Remove pan sides. Place pie in an airtight container and store overnight. Before serving, dust lightly with powdered sugar. Makes 8 servings.

Custard Tart

1/2 recipe Short-Crust
 Pastry, page 86
1 egg white, lightly beaten
3 eggs
2 tablespoons superfine
 sugar
1-1/4 cups milk
1/4 teaspoon vanilla extract
Ground nutmeg to taste

A traditional English favorite, this delicate-flavored tart is light yet satisfying. And yes, it is called a "tart" even though it is baked in a pie pan. (If you have trouble with custard or other liquid fillings soaking into pastry and making it soggy, brush the pie shell with a little beaten egg white before baking the pastry.)

Preheat oven to 400F (205C). Grease an 8-inch pie pan. On a lightly floured surface, thinly roll out pastry with a floured rolling pin. Line pie pan with pastry; brush lightly with egg white. Bake 10 minutes or until pastry is just set. Set aside on a wire rack to cool. In a medium-size bowl, beat together eggs, sugar, milk and vanilla. Pour gently into pastry shell. Sprinkle top with nutmeg. Bake 5 minutes; reduce oven temperature to 350F (175C) and bake 15 minutes longer or until custard is set. Cool in pan on a wire rack. Serve cold. Makes 8 servings.

Variation
Raisin Custard Tart: Sprinkle 1/2 cup raisins on bottom of pie shell before pouring in egg mixture.

Grapefruit Meringue Tart

1/2 recipe Rich Short-Crust
  Pastry, page 86
1 tablespoon unsalted butter
1/4 cup cornstarch
1-1/4 cups water
Finely grated peel and juice
  of 1 medium grapefruit
1/2 cup superfine sugar
2 egg yolks

Meringue:
2 egg whites, room
  temperature
4 tablespoons superfine
  sugar

This is a delicious change from the more common lemon meringue pie.

Preheat oven to 425F (220C). Grease an 8-inch fluted tart pan with a removable bottom. On a lightly floured surface, thinly roll out pastry with a floured rolling pin. Line tart pan with pastry; prick bottom of tart shell lightly with a fork. Line bottom and sides of shell with a circle of parchment paper. Fill shell with uncooked beans or rice or with pie weights. Bake 15 minutes. Remove beans and paper; bake tart shell 15 minutes longer or until pale golden. Set aside on a wire rack to cool. Reduce oven temperature to 325F (165C). In a medium-size saucepan, combine butter, cornstarch, water, grapefruit peel and juice and 1/2 cup superfine sugar. Bring to a boil over medium heat, stirring constantly with a wire whisk or wooden spoon. Reduce heat and stir 2 minutes longer. Remove from heat and cool 5 minutes. Beat in egg yolks; set aside. For meringue: in a medium-size bowl, beat egg whites until stiff peaks form. Gradually add 2 tablespoons sugar and beat until meringue is very stiff. Gently fold in remaining 2 tablespoons superfine sugar. Pour grapefruit mixture into tart shell. Spoon meringue gently over filling and spread to edge of crust, sealing completely. Swirl top with a knife. Bake 15 to 20 minutes or until meringue is light golden brown. Remove pan sides before serving. Serve warm or cold. Makes 8 servings.

Variation
The above recipe will give a soft meringue. If you prefer a drier, crisper texture, bake tart at 200F (95C) 1 to 1-1/2 hours.

Lemon Curd Tart

1/2 recipe Sweet Short-Crust
  Pastry, page 87
2 tablespoons raspberry jam
1/4 cup lemon curd,
  homemade, page 155, or
  purchased
1/2 pint (1 cup) whipping
  cream

Lemon curd is a very common English preserve. It's sold in jars in import or specialty stores, or you can also make it at home. This unusual tart looks impressive, but it's quick and easy.

Preheat oven to 425F (220C). Grease an 8-inch fluted tart pan with a removable bottom. On a lightly floured surface, thinly roll out pastry with a floured rolling pin. Line tart pan with pastry; prick bottom of tart shell with a fork. Line bottom of shell with a circle of parchment paper. Fill shell with uncooked beans or rice or with pie weights. Bake 15 minutes. Remove beans and paper; bake tart shell 15 minutes longer until pastry is light golden. Remove from pan and place shell on rack to cool completely. Transfer shell to serving plate. Spread shell with jam, then cover with lemon curd. In a medium-size bowl, beat cream until it holds stiff peaks. Spread over lemon curd. Makes 8 servings.

Drunken Plum Tart

1 recipe Pâte Brisée, page 88
2 eggs
1/4 cup ground almonds
1/4 cup sugar
5 tablespoons whipping
   cream
1/4 cup brandy
1 teaspoon vanilla extract
1 teaspoon water
1 tablespoon butter, melted,
   cooled
2 pounds ripe plums, halved,
   pitted

Serve this sophisticated tart in thin wedges—plain for afternoon tea or topped with whipped cream at high tea.

Preheat oven to 425F (220C). Grease a 9-inch fluted tart pan with a removable bottom. On a lightly floured surface, thinly roll out pastry with a floured rolling pin. Line tart pan with pastry; lightly prick bottom of tart shell with a fork. Set aside. In a medium-size bowl, lightly beat eggs. Thoroughly mix in almonds, sugar, cream, brandy, vanilla and water. Stir in melted butter. Arrange plums cut-side down in tart shell. Pour almond mixture over fruit; carefully smooth top. Bake about 25 minutes or until filling is set and plums are soft when pierced with a wooden pick. Cool in pan on a wire rack. Remove pan sides before serving. Serve warm or cold. Makes 8 servings.

Tropical Apple Tart

1/2 recipe Short-Crust
   Pastry, page 86
1-1/2 cups unsweetened
   pineapple juice
3/4 cup sugar
6 large tart apples, peeled,
   cored, thickly sliced
3 tablespoons cornstarch
1 tablespoon butter
1/2 teaspoon vanilla extract

This one-crust pie is a great summertime apple treat.

Preheat oven to 425F (220C). Grease a 9-inch fluted tart pan with a removable bottom. On a lightly floured surface, thinly roll out pastry with a floured rolling pin. Line tart pan with pastry; prick bottom of tart shell lightly with a fork. Line bottom and sides of shell with a circle of parchment paper. Fill shell with uncooked beans or rice or with pie weights. Bake 15 minutes. Remove beans and paper; bake tart shell 15 minutes longer or until pale golden. Set aside on a wire rack to cool. In a medium-size saucepan, combine 1-1/4 cups pineapple juice and the sugar. Bring to a boil, stirring until sugar is dissolved. Add apples, reduce heat, cover and simmer 3 to 4 minutes or until apples are tender but not mushy. With a slotted spoon, lift apples from liquid and set aside to drain in a colander; reserve liquid. In a small bowl, stir together cornstarch and remaining 1/4 cup pineapple juice. Pour into hot liquid and cook over medium heat, stirring, until mixture bubbles and starts to thicken. Cook 1 minute longer. Remove from heat. Stir in butter and vanilla until butter is melted. Cover and set aside to cool 30 minutes. (Do not stir during this time; stirring interferes with thickening.) Pour 1/2 of cooled pineapple juice mixture into tart shell, spreading evenly to cover bottom. Attractively arrange apple slices on top. Spoon remaining pineapple juice mixture over apples. Cover with foil and refrigerate at least 1 hour. Remove pan sides before serving. Makes 8 servings.

A ground almond, cream and brandy mixture, poured over a plum-filled pastry shell, gives Drunken Plum Tart its apt title.

Bakewell Tart

1/2 recipe Sweet Short-Crust
  Pastry, page 87
2 tablespoons raspberry jam
1-1/2 cups fine, soft, light
  cake crumbs
3/4 cup ground almonds
1/4 cup butter, room
  temperature
1/4 cup sugar
Grated peel of 1/2 lemon
1 egg
Juice of 1/2 lemon (about 2
  tablespoons), as needed

This tart doesn't get its name from the way it's cooked! It's called after the small Derbyshire town where it originated. For the cake crumbs, use sponge, pound or any other light—not chocolate—cake.

Preheat oven to 425F (220C). Grease an 8-inch fluted tart pan with a removable bottom. On a lightly floured surface, thinly roll out pastry with a floured rolling pin. Line tart pan with pastry. Spread bottom of tart shell with jam. Set aside. In a medium-size bowl, mix cake crumbs and almonds; set aside. In a large bowl, cream butter, sugar and lemon peel with an electric mixer or a wooden spoon until light and fluffy. Beat in egg. Fold in almond mixture. Add lemon juice as needed until mixture is soft enough to drop from a spoon but too thick to pour. Turn mixture into tart shell; smooth top. Bake 15 minutes; reduce oven temperature to 350F (175C) and bake 20 to 30 minutes or until pastry is browned and filling springs back when lightly touched. Remove pan sides before serving. Serve warm or cold. Makes 8 servings.

Tartlets and Small Pastries

For larger parties, individual tartlets or other small pastries are much easier to handle than plate-size tarts. Whatever the filling—sweet or savory—this particular category of tasty delights is always welcome at a tea party.

Coventry Tartlets

1/2 recipe Short-Crust
  Pastry, page 86
1 (8-oz.) package (1/2-lb.)
  cream cheese, room
  temperature
1/2 cup sugar
1/4 cup butter, room
  temperature
2 egg yolks
Pinch of salt
1/4 teaspoon ground nutmeg
1 tablespoon orange juice

These little tarts come from Coventry, a city in the midlands of England where, among other things, Lady Godiva took her famous ride.

Preheat oven to 450F (230C). Grease 12 (2-inch) tartlet pans or muffin cups. On a lightly floured surface, thinly roll out pastry with a floured rolling pin. Cut into rounds with a 3-inch cookie cutter. Line pans with pastry; prick bottoms lightly with a fork. Set aside. In a medium-size bowl, combine cream cheese, sugar, butter, egg yolks, salt, nutmeg and orange juice. Beat with a wooden spoon or an electric mixer until smooth. Divide among pastry shells; smooth tops. Bake 10 minutes; reduce oven temperature to 325F (165C) and bake 10 minutes longer or until golden brown and firm to the touch. Carefully remove from pans and cool on a wire rack. Makes 12 tartlets.

Fruit Tartlets, page 96, are an elegant inclusion on any tea table. The simple application of a warmed jelly glaze, lightly brushed over the top of the fruit, gives the pastries a quite professional-looking finish with just a modicum of effort.

Fruit Tartlets

1 recipe Rich Short-Crust
  Pastry, page 86
Fresh or canned fruit (see
  suggestions in recipe
  introduction)
1/2 cup apricot, apple,
  raspberry or red currant
  jelly, as appropriate

Just about any variety of fruit is delicious in these tartlets. The exact amount will depend upon availability and size so I am unable to be specific in my recommendations. In summer, use fresh strawberries, raspberries, blueberries, cherries, apricots, peaches or kiwifruit. Stem, pit and peel fruit as appropriate, and slice larger fruits, such as peaches. In winter or when fresh fruit is not available, use canned fruit of your choice or fresh orange segments. Drain canned fruit thoroughly before using.

The jelly used to glaze tartlets depends on the fruit. For light-colored fruit, use apricot or apple jelly; for red and other dark-colored fruit, use raspberry or red currant jelly.

Preheat oven to 400F (205C). Grease 12 (2-inch) tartlet pans or muffin cups. On a lightly floured surface, thinly roll out pastry with a floured rolling pin. Cut into 12 rounds with a 3-inch cookie cutter. Line pans with pastry; prick bottoms lightly with a fork. Bake about 10 minutes or until golden brown. Carefully remove from pans and cool completely on a wire rack. Arrange fruit attractively in pastry shells. In a small saucepan, stir jelly over low heat just until melted. Using a pastry brush, glaze fruit completely with jelly. Cool before serving. Makes 12 tartlets.

Maids of Honor

1 recipe Rich Short-Crust
  Pastry, page 86
1/4 cup butter, room
  temperature
1/4 cup granulated sugar
1 egg
1 teaspoon brandy
1/2 cup all-purpose flour,
  sifted
3 tablespoons powdered
  sugar

These small tarts originated in Henry VIII's palace at Hampton Court, where they were popular with the queen's maids of honor. The recipe, kept a closely guarded secret for centuries, was finally revealed in 1951 on a television program about historic dishes of England. The original recipe calls for curdling milk with rennet to make flavored curds—a tricky and time-consuming process. Here is a simpler but no less delicious version.

Preheat oven to 350F (175C). Grease 12 (2-inch) tartlet pans or muffin cups. On a lightly floured surface, thinly roll out pastry with a floured rolling pin. Cut into 12 rounds with a 3-inch cookie cutter. Line pans with pastry. In a medium-size bowl, cream butter and granulated sugar with an electric mixer or a wooden spoon until light and fluffy. Beat in egg; stir in brandy. Gently but thoroughly fold in flour. Spoon mixture into pastry shells. Bake 20 to 25 minutes or until pastry is browned and filling springs back when lightly touched. Carefully remove from pans and cool on a wire rack. Dust with powdered sugar before serving. Makes 12 tartlets.

Cherry Tartlets

1 recipe Pâte Sucrée,
  page 88
1 pound tart red cherries,
  stemmed, pitted
2 tablespoons granulated
  sugar
2 eggs, separated
2 tablespoons superfine
  sugar

These mouthwatering tartlets are adapted from a recipe in an English cookbook dated 1923.

Preheat oven to 400F (205C). Grease 12 deep (2-inch) tartlet pans or muffin cups. On a lightly floured surface, thinly roll out pastry with a floured rolling pin. Cut into 12 rounds with a 3-inch cookie cutter. Line pans with pastry; prick bottoms lightly with a fork. Bake about 10 minutes or until golden brown. Cool tartlet shells in pans on a wire rack. Meanwhile, combine cherries and granulated sugar in a narrow-mouthed 1-quart glass canning jar. Set jar in a large saucepan of boiling water. (Or place cherries and sugar in the top of a small double boiler over simmering water.) Cook, uncovered, about 30 minutes or until cherries are tender. Remove from heat and carefully strain cherry syrup into top of a small double boiler. Set cherries aside. (If cherries are cooked in double boiler, carefully remove with a slotted spoon, leaving as much of the syrup as possible in the pan.) Beat egg yolks into syrup, then stir over barely simmering water until custard is thickened. Set custard aside. In a medium-size bowl, beat egg whites until stiff peaks form. Divide cherries among pastry shells. Cover with a layer of custard. Top tarts with egg white; sprinkle each with 1/2 teaspoon superfine sugar. Return to oven about 4 minutes or until meringue is set and lightly browned. Carefully remove from pans. Serve warm or cold. Makes 12 tartlets.

Iced Hazelnut Tartlets

1 recipe Sweet Short-Crust
  Pastry, page 87
1 tablespoon all-purpose
  flour, sifted
1/4 cup fine, soft, light cake
  crumbs
1/4 cup finely chopped
  hazelnuts
2 tablespoons butter, room
  temperature
1/4 cup superfine sugar
1 egg
1-1/2 tablespoons milk
1 teaspoon honey
About 2 tablespoons
  raspberry jam

Coffee Icing:
1/2 cup powdered sugar
1-1/2 tablespoons cold coffee

A coffee-flavored glaze gives these rich little tarts a sophisticated air.

Preheat oven to 400F (205C). Grease 12 (2-inch) tartlet pans or muffin cups. On a lightly floured surface, thinly roll out pastry with a floured rolling pin. Cut into 12 rounds with a 3-inch cookie cutter. Line pans with pastry. Sift flour into a medium-size bowl; mix in cake crumbs and hazelnuts. Set aside. In another medium-size bowl, cream butter and sugar until light and fluffy. Beat in egg, milk and honey. Fold in hazelnut mixture and blend well. Put about 1/2 teaspoon jam in bottom of each pastry shell. Spoon filling over jam, smoothing tops. Bake 15 to 20 minutes or until filling is firm. Remove from pans and cool completely on a wire rack. Prepare Coffee Icing. Spread over tartlets. Makes 12 tartlets.

Coffee Icing:
Combine sugar with coffee in a small bowl and mix until smooth.

Banbury Tarts

1 cup raisins, chopped
1 cup superfine sugar
3 tablespoons fine dry bread crumbs or cracker crumbs
1 egg, beaten
1 tablespoon butter, melted, cooled
Pinch of salt
Grated peel of 1 lemon
Juice of 1 lemon (about 1/4 cup)
1-1/2 sheets (14" x 11") frozen puff pastry, thawed but still cold

These little melt-in-the-mouth turnovers are a regional specialty.

Preheat oven to 450F (230C). Grease a large baking sheet; set aside. In a large bowl, combine raisins, superfine sugar, bread crumbs, egg, melted butter, salt, lemon peel and lemon juice; mix well. Set aside. Set pastry on a lightly floured surface. With a sharp knife, cut in 3-inch squares. Gently work trimmings together and re-roll with floured rolling pin. Cut into additional squares. Divide fruit mixture among pastry squares. Dampen edges of each square; fold squares in half diagonally to form a triangle and press edges to seal. With a sharp knife, cut 2 short slits in top of each triangle. Place pastries on baking sheet. Bake about 15 minutes or until golden brown. Transfer to a wire rack to cool. Makes about 24 pastries.

Apple Turnovers

2 large tart apples, peeled, cored, finely diced
1 tablespoon packed light brown sugar
1/2 teaspoon ground cinnamon
1 teaspoon lemon juice
1 sheet (14" x 11") frozen puff pastry, thawed but still cold
1 egg white, lightly beaten
3 tablespoons superfine sugar

These are simple, homey and absolutely wonderful for a winter tea.

In a medium-size bowl, toss together apples, brown sugar, cinnamon and lemon juice; set aside. Rinse a large baking sheet with cold water; shake off excess water but leave baking sheet damp. Set pastry on a lightly floured surface. With a sharp knife, cut pastry lengthwise into 3 equal strips; then cut crosswise into squares (there will be some leftover pastry). Put 1/9 of apple mixture in center of each square. Dampen edges of each square; fold squares in half diagonally to make a triangle and press edges to seal. With a sharp knife, cut 2 short slits in top of each turnover. Place on baking sheet and refrigerate 30 minutes. Meanwhile, preheat oven to 425F (220C). Brush turnovers with egg white and sprinkle with superfine sugar. Bake about 20 minutes or until crisp and golden. Transfer to a wire rack to cool. Serve warm or cold. Makes 9 turnovers.

Pastry Windmills, touched with a dollop of raspberry jam and dipped in powdered sugar, add a note of whimsy to tea time.

Pastry Windmills

**1/2 recipe Rich Short-Crust
  Pastry, page 86
1/4 cup raspberry jam
1/4 cup powdered sugar**

Though these little pastries sound childishly simple, they look most elegant when arranged on your tea table.

 Preheat oven to 450F (230C). Grease a large baking sheet; set aside. On a lightly floured surface, roll out pastry with a floured rolling pin into a rectangle about 9" x 12". With a sharp knife, cut in 3-inch squares; cut squares diagonally from each corner toward center, making cuts about 1 inch long. Put 1 teaspoon jam in center of each square. Fold corners toward center, overlapping them slightly so pastry looks like a windmill. Arrange on baking sheet. Bake about 12 minutes or until golden. Transfer to a wire rack to cool. Before serving, dust lightly with powdered sugar. Makes 12 windmills.

Raspberry jam and chopped nutmeats, spread and sprinkled over a sweet short-crust pastry, are easily made—and quickly consumed.

Nut Rolls

1 recipe Sweet Short-Crust Pastry, page 87
1/2 cup raspberry jam
1/2 cup finely chopped walnuts or hazelnuts
1/4 cup powdered sugar

Very simple to make, these are nevertheless both good-looking and delicious.

Preheat oven to 450F (230C). Grease a large baking sheet; set aside. On a lightly floured surface, thinly roll out pastry with a floured rolling pin. Cut in rounds with a 4-inch cookie cutter. Prick each round lightly with a fork. Spread lightly with jam and sprinkle with nuts. Tightly roll up each round and place seam-side down on baking sheet. Bake about 15 minutes or until golden. Transfer to a wire rack to cool. Before serving, dust with powdered sugar. Makes about 10 pastries.

Variation
Instead of dusting rolls with powdered sugar, drizzle with melted unsweetened chocolate.

Marmalade Sandwiches

1/2 recipe Sweet Short-Crust
   Pastry, page 87
1/2 cup orange marmalade
Orange Icing (recipe
   follows)
1/4 cup chopped walnuts
Orange Icing:
1/2 cup powdered sugar
1-1/2 tablespoons orange
   juice

These simple pastries are filled with marmalade rather than the more typically used jam. If you like, use Amber Marmalade, page 152.

Preheat oven to 400F (205C). Grease a medium-size nonstick baking sheet. Divide pastry in half. On a lightly floured surface, roll each portion of pastry with a floured rolling pin into a rectangle about 1/8 inch thick (each rectangle should be about 4" x 10"). Carefully transfer 1 rectangle to baking sheet. Spread almost to edges with marmalade. Top with remaining rectangle. With a sharp knife, carefully cut pastry into fingers about 2" x 4"; separate slightly. Bake about 15 minutes or until golden brown. Transfer to a wire rack to cool completely. Prepare Orange Icing. Spread over pastries, then sprinkle with walnuts. Makes about 10 pastries.

Orange Icing:
Combine sugar and orange juice in a small bowl and mix until smooth.

Blueberry Tartlets

1 recipe Rich Short-Crust
   Pastry, page 86
2 (3-oz.) packages cream
   cheese, room temperature
1/4 cup half-and-half
1 tablespoon superfine sugar
1/2 cup fresh blueberries,
   washed and dried
3/4 cup red currant or grape
   jelly

These delectible tartlets taste almost like mini cheesecakes.

Preheat oven to 400F (205C). Grease 12 (2-inch) tartlet pans or muffin cups. On a lighty floured surface, thinly roll out pastry with a floured rolling pin. Cut in 12 rounds with a 3-inch cookie cutter. Line pans with pastry; prick bottoms lightly with a fork. Bake about 10 minutes or until golden brown. Carefully remove from pans and cool completely on a wire rack. In a food processor or blender, or in a medium bowl with a wooden spoon, combine cream cheese, half-and-half and sugar and mix until light and fluffy. Divide among pastry shells, smoothing tops. Sprinkle blueberries over filling. In a small saucepan, stir jelly over low heat until just melted. Drizzle about 1 tablespoon jelly over berries. Refrigerate until jelly is set. Serve chilled. Makes 12 tartlets.

Cakes

Cake-making is an evolution of bread-making. Early on, adventurous cooks experimented by adding extra fat, or perhaps dried fruit, to make something a little different and special. And cake for tea is *still* special. The addition of eggs and then, in this century, various rising ingredients, have transformed the preparation of this dessert into the fine art it is today.

You will find many of these teatime recipes—for both large and small cakes—a little drier than the very moist, almost pudding-like cakes you might enjoy after dinner. This texture seems to compliment tea and be the perfect choice for afternoon.

A large cake on an attractive plate or cake stand makes a wonderful centerpiece for your tea table. Layer cakes, sponge cakes and rich fruitcakes are usually served for afternoon tea; elaborate, creamy gâteaux aren't generally appropriate unless you're celebrating a special occasion like a birthday or holiday. Serve your afternoon tea cake in small slivers, not as big as those you'd dish up for after-dinner dessert.

Queen of Chocolate Cake

9 ounces semisweet chocolate, chopped *or* 1-1/2 (6-oz.) packages (1-1/2 cups) semisweet chocolate pieces
1/2 cup unsalted butter, room temperature
3/4 cup superfine sugar
1/2 teaspoon vanilla extract
6 eggs, separated
1 tablespoon all-purpose flour
Pinch of cream of tartar

Chocolate Frosting:
6 ounces semisweet chocolate, chopped *or* 1 (6-oz.) package (1 cup) semisweet chocolate pieces
2 eggs
1/2 cup unsalted butter, room temperature

Moist and chocolaty, this is about as rich as a teacake should ever get.

Preheat oven to 450F (230C). Grease an 8-inch springform pan. Line with parchment paper; grease paper and dust lightly with flour. Set aside. Melt chocolate in the top of a double boiler over simmering water; remove from heat but leave over hot water to keep warm. In a large bowl, cream butter and superfine sugar with an electric mixer or a wooden spoon until light and fluffy. Beat in chocolate and vanilla. Add egg yolks 1 at a time and beat until well mixed. Beat in flour. Cover and refrigerate. In another large bowl, beat egg whites with cream of tartar until stiff peaks form. Remove chocolate mixture from refrigerator and gently mix in about 1/3 of egg whites to loosen batter. Fold in remaining egg whites. Pour into cake pan. Bake 5 minutes. Reduce oven temperature to 300F (150C) and continue baking about 30 minutes longer or until a wooden pick inserted 2 inches from side of pan comes out clean (center should remain a little sticky). Cool in pan about 15 minutes. Carefully remove pan sides and turn out cake onto a wire rack. Peel off paper and allow cake to cool completely. Meanwhile, prepare Chocolate Frosting. Spread over top and sides of cake. Pipe some of frosting decoratively on cake, if desired. Makes 8 to 10 servings.

Chocolate Frosting:
Melt chocolate in the top of a double boiler over simmering water. Remove from heat but leave over hot water to keep warm. In a large bowl, beat eggs and butter until well mixed. Beat in chocolate until mixture is fluffy. Cover and refrigerate about 30 minutes until firm but spreadable before frosting cake.

On the preceding pages: Arrange the refreshments for an elegant tea in a sunny window, set off with some of your loveliest finery. Oven Scones, page 67, frothy Syllabub, page 130, and Queen of Chocolate Cake, above, make a memorable tea indeed.

Applesauce Cake

4 cups all-purpose flour
1 tablespoon ground cloves
2 teaspoons ground
  cinnamon
1 teaspoon ground ginger
1/2 teaspoon ground nutmeg
1 cup butter or margarine,
  room temperature
1 cup granulated sugar
1 cup packed light brown
  sugar
2 cups unsweetened
  applesauce
2 cups raisins
2 teaspoons baking soda
1/4 cup hot water

Moist and spicy, this big tube cake is a wonderful choice for an autumn tea.

⚮ Preheat oven to 350F (175C). Generously grease a 10-inch tube pan; set aside. Sift flour, cloves, cinnamon, ginger and nutmeg into a large bowl; set aside. In another large bowl, cream butter and sugars with an electric mixer or a wooden spoon until light and fluffy. Mix in applesauce. Add dry ingredients and beat until smooth. Stir in raisins. Dissolve baking soda in hot water; stir into batter. Pour into pan. Bake about 1 hour or until a wooden pick inserted in center comes out clean. Cool in pan about 5 minutes, then turn out onto a wire rack to cool completely. Makes 12 to 16 servings.

Scottish Ginger Cake

3 cups all-purpose flour
1/2 teaspoon salt
2 teaspoons baking soda
1 tablespoon ground ginger
1/3 cup golden raisins
1/3 cup chopped mixed
  candied peel
1/3 cup crystallized ginger,
  chopped
3/4 cup molasses
3/4 cup butter
1/3 cup packed brown sugar
3 eggs, beaten
2 to 3 tablespoons milk

A rich, stick-to-the-ribs cake from north of the border, this improves with keeping in an airtight tin. Don't serve it to guests on a diet!

⚮ Preheat oven to 325F (165C). Generously grease an 8-inch square baking pan; set aside. Sift flour, salt, baking soda and ground ginger into a large bowl. Stir in raisins, candied peel and crystallized ginger; set aside. In a medium-size saucepan, combine molasses, butter and brown sugar. Stir over low heat until butter is melted. Remove from heat. Beat in eggs and milk. Make a well in center of dry ingredients. Pour in molasses mixture and beat thoroughly. Pour into cake pan. Bake 1-1/4 hours or until top springs back when lightly touched with finger. Cool in pan on a wire rack. Makes 8 to 12 servings.

Victoria Sandwich Sponge

1-1/2 cups self-rising flour
Grated peel of 1-1/2 lemons
3/4 cup butter or margarine,
    room temperature
3/4 cup granulated sugar
3 eggs
1/3 cup (or more) strawberry
    jam
Powdered sugar

This light cake is a teatime classic for all seasons. For an especially attractive Victoria sandwich, place a pretty paper doily on top of the cake before sifting with powdered sugar. Very carefully remove the doily and the cake will have a lacy pattern stenciled on top.

Preheat oven to 350F (175C). Grease 2 round 8-inch cake pans; set aside. Sift flour into a small bowl; stir in lemon peel. Set aside. In a large bowl, cream butter and granulated sugar with an electric mixer or a wooden spoon until light and fluffy. Beat in eggs 1 at a time. Fold in flour mixture. Divide batter between pans, spreading evenly. Bake 25 minutes or until top of cake springs back when lightly touched. Cool in pans a few minutes, then turn out onto wire racks to cool completely. To serve, sandwich layers together with jam and sift powdered sugar over top. Makes 8 to 10 servings.

Mocha Layer Cake

1-3/4 cups all-purpose flour
1 tablespoon baking powder
1/2 cup unsweetened cocoa
    powder
1/2 teaspoon salt
1/2 cup butter or margarine,
    room temperature
1 cup superfine sugar
1 teaspoon vanilla extract
6 egg yolks
3/4 cup milk

Mocha Filling:
1/2 cup unsalted butter,
    room temperature
1 cup powdered sugar
About 2 tablespoons very
    strong coffee, cooled

The classic combination of coffee and chocolate gives this moist cake its wonderful flavor.

Preheat oven to 350F (175C). Grease and lightly flour 2 round 9-inch cake pans; set aside. Sift flour, baking powder, cocoa and salt into a medium-size bowl; set aside. In a large bowl, cream butter and superfine sugar with an electric mixer or a wooden spoon until light and fluffy. Stir in vanilla. In a medium-size bowl, beat egg yolks on high speed of electric mixer until very thick and creamy (about the consistency of thin mayonnaise, about 10 minutes). Beat into butter mixture. Add dry ingredients alternately with milk, beating until smooth after each addition. Divide batter between pans; smooth tops. Bake about 25 minutes or until top of cake springs back when lightly touched. Cool in pans a few minutes, then turn out onto wire racks to cool completely. Prepare Mocha Filling. Sandwich layers together with filling. Makes 8 to 10 servings.

Mocha Filling:
In a medium-size bowl, cream butter and powdered sugar with electric mixer until light and smooth. Add coffee, a little at a time, and mix until filling is spreadable.

Victoria Sandwich Sponge, filled with strawberry jam and decorated with a lacy pattern of sifted powdered sugar, is topped with a single white chocolate-dipped strawberry, page 128,—and served with more!

Battenberg Cake

1/2 cup butter or margarine, room temperature
1 cup superfine sugar
3 eggs
1/2 teaspoon vanilla extract
1-1/2 cups self-rising flour, sifted
About 2 drops red food coloring
Marzipan (recipe follows)
About 1/2 cup raspberry jam
Powdered sugar

Marzipan:
2 cups finely ground blanched almonds
2 cups powdered sugar
1 cup granulated sugar
1 teaspoon lemon juice
1/2 teaspoon almond extract
1/2 teaspoon vanilla extract
1 egg, lightly beaten
1 egg yolk, lightly beaten, if needed

A pink and white "checkerboard" wrapped in marzipan, Battenberg Cake brings showy elegance to your tea table. The recipe probably originated with the English and German royal families in the early 20th century.

Preheat oven to 375F (190C). Grease a 12" x 8" baking pan. Line pan with parchment paper, pleating paper lengthwise to make a "wall" down center of pan; grease paper. Set pan aside. In a large bowl, cream butter and superfine sugar with an electric mixer or a wooden spoon until light and fluffy. Beat in eggs 1 at a time. Beat in vanilla. Fold in flour. Pour 1/2 of batter into 1 side of pan; smooth top. Add food coloring to remaining batter and blend well. Pour into other side of pan and smooth top. Bake 40 to 45 minutes or until top springs back when lightly touched. Cool cake in pan a few minutes, then carefully turn out of pan onto a wire rack and peel off paper. Cool cakes completely. Meanwhile, prepare Marzipan; set aside. To assemble, trim sides and tops of white and pink cakes flat. Cut each cake in half lengthwise to make a total of 4 (2" x 12") rectangles. Sandwich all 4 rectangles together with jam, alternating white and pink pieces for a checkerboard effect. Spread top, bottom and sides of cake lightly with jam. Turn out marzipan onto a surface dusted lightly with powdered sugar. Using rolling pin covered with powdered sugar, roll marzipan 1/8-inch thick about 12 inches long and wide enough to completely wrap top, bottom and sides—not ends—of cake. Carefully wrap cake in marzipan, pressing gently to adhere to cake. With your thumb and forefinger, pinch seams together to seal; trim off any excess marzipan. To serve, cut cake crosswise in slices. Makes 8 to 10 servings.

Marzipan:
In a large bowl, mix almonds, powdered sugar, granulated sugar, lemon juice, almond extract, vanilla and egg to form a soft paste. If necessary, mix in egg yolk to give marzipan the correct consistency.

Golden Marmalade Cake

3 cups all-purpose flour
4 teaspoons baking powder
1/2 teaspoon salt
1/2 cup butter, room temperature
1-1/2 cups sugar
6 egg yolks
1 teaspoon vanilla extract
1 cup milk
1/4 cup orange marmalade

A rich sandwich cake filled with tangy orange marmalade.

Preheat oven to 375F (190C). Grease 2 round 8-inch cake pans; set aside. Sift flour, baking powder and salt into a medium-size bowl; set aside. In a large bowl, cream butter and sugar with an electric mixer or a wooden spoon until light and fluffy. Beat in egg yolks 1 at a time. Stir in vanilla. Alternately add dry ingredients and milk, beating until smooth after each addition. Pour into layer pans; smooth tops. Bake 20 to 25 minutes or until top of cake springs back when lightly touched. Cool in pans a few minutes, then turn out onto wire racks to cool completely. Sandwich layers together with marmalade. Makes 8 to 10 servings.

Marble Cake never looks the same twice. A mixture of white and chocolate batters, lightly swirled together, creates the abstract design.

Marble Cake

2 cups self-rising flour
1/2 cup butter or margarine,
   room temperature
3/4 cup sugar
2 eggs
1 teaspoon vanilla extract
4 tablespoons milk
2 tablespoons unsweetened
   cocoa powder
2 tablespoons water

An impressive-looking cake that's surprisingly simple to make.

Preheat oven to 350F (175C). Grease a round 2-inch-deep, 9-inch-diameter cake pan; set aside. Sift flour into a medium-size bowl; set aside. In a large bowl, cream butter and sugar with an electric mixer or a wooden spoon until light and fluffy. Beat in eggs 1 at a time; beat in vanilla. Alternately add flour and milk, beating until smooth after each addition. Pour half of batter into another bowl. Stir together cocoa and water; beat into 1 bowl of batter. Add alternate spoonfuls of light and chocolate batter to cake pan; gently swirl together with a fork. Bake 35 to 40 minutes or until a wooden pick inserted in center comes out clean. Cool cake in pan a few minutes, then turn out onto a wire rack to cool completely. Makes 8 to 10 servings.

Dundee Cake

2 cups all-purpose flour
1-1/2 teaspoons baking
 powder
3/4 cup butter or margarine,
 room temperature
3/4 cup sugar
3 eggs
2-2/3 cups diced mixed dried
 fruit
1/4 cup candied cherries
1/3 cup chopped mixed
 candied peel
1 tablespoon brandy
1/2 cup blanched almonds
1 egg white, lightly beaten

It seems that some of the heartiest and most aromatic cakes come from Scotland, perhaps because the harsh weather invites such indulgences. This cake, named for a Scottish city, is wonderful for a winter tea. Rich and fruity, it could easily be used as a Christmas cake, if you like.

Preheat oven to 325F (165C). Grease a round 2-inch-deep, 8-inch-diameter cake pan; set aside. Sift flour and baking powder into a medium-size bowl. In a large bowl, cream butter and sugar with an electric mixer or a wooden spoon until light and fluffy. Beat in eggs 1 at a time. Fold in dry ingredients. Stir in dried fruit, cherries and candied peel. Stir in brandy and mix well (batter should be soft). Pour into pan; smooth top. Arrange almonds over top in concentric circles. Brush almonds with egg white. Bake 1-1/2 hours. Reduce oven temperature to 300F (150C) and bake 30 to 40 minutes longer or until a wooden pick inserted in center comes out clean. Cool in pan 1 hour, then turn out onto a wire rack to cool completely. Makes 8 to 10 servings.

Madeira Cake

2 cups all-purpose flour
1/2 cup rice flour
1 teaspoon cream of tartar
1 teaspoon baking soda
1/4 teaspoon salt
4 eggs
Juice of 1/2 lemon (about 2
 tablespoons)
1/2 cup butter or margarine,
 room temperature
1/2 cup superfine sugar
2 or 3 slices candied citron
 or thin slices candied
 orange or lemon peel

Richer than the Victoria sandwich, this lemony cake is also a teatime favorite. You will notice that the oven door is opened midway through the baking time in order to add the citron garnish. I assure you this is correct and the cake will not suffer from such an unusual technique.

Preheat oven to 350F (175C). Grease a round 2-inch-deep, 8-inch diameter cake pan; set aside. Sift flours, cream of tartar, baking soda and salt into a medium-size bowl; set aside. In a small bowl, lightly beat eggs; stir in lemon juice. In a large bowl, cream butter and superfine sugar with an electric mixer or a wooden spoon until light and fluffy. Alternately add dry ingredients and egg mixture, beating until smooth after each addition. Pour into pan, smoothing top. Bake 30 minutes. Arrange citron on top of cake. Bake 30 minutes longer or until a wooden pick inserted in center comes out clean. Cool in pan a few minutes, then turn out of pan onto a wire rack to cool completely. Makes 8 to 10 servings.

Scottish Dundee Cake, filled with dried fruits and topped with blanched almonds, is especially welcome for a winter tea.

Caramel Cake

2 tablespoons Caramel Syrup
(recipe follows)
2-1/2 cups all-purpose flour
2 teaspoons baking powder
1/2 teaspoon salt
1/2 cup butter or margarine,
room temperature
1-1/2 cups sugar
2 eggs
1 teaspoon vanilla extract
1 cup milk
Caramel Filling (recipe
follows)

Caramel Syrup:
1/2 cup sugar
1/2 cup boiling water

Caramel Filling:
1-1/2 cups packed light
brown sugar
1 tablespoon butter or
margarine
2 tablespoons cornstarch
1 cup milk
1-1/2 teaspoons vanilla
extract

Though it takes a little time to make, this cake is well worth the effort.

Prepare Caramel Syrup; measure out 2 tablespoons to use in cake (refrigerate remainder to use another time). Preheat oven to 375F (190C). Grease 2 round 8-inch cake pans; set aside. Sift flour, baking powder and salt into a medium-size bowl; set aside. In a large bowl, cream butter and sugar with an electric mixer or a wooden spoon until light and fluffy. Beat in eggs 1 at a time. Add vanilla and Caramel Syrup and mix well. Alternately add dry ingredients and milk, beating only enough to blend ingredients thoroughly after each addition. Divide batter between pans; smooth tops. Bake about 20 minutes or until top of cake springs back when lightly touched. Cool layers in pans a few minutes, then turn out onto wire racks to cool completely. While cake is cooling, prepare Caramel Filling. Sandwich layers together with filling. Makes 8 to 10 servings.

Caramel Syrup:
Pour sugar into a small, heavy saucepan. Place over low heat until sugar starts to melt, shaking pan frequently. Continue heating until sugar starts to smoke slightly. Add boiling water—*be careful because it will spatter*—and stir to mix well. Allow to boil until a heavy syrup is formed. Time varies according to heat as well as size and weight of saucepan so watch carefully.

Caramel Filling
Combine brown sugar, butter, cornstarch and milk in the top of a double boiler. Cook over simmering water until mixture is thickened, stirring frequently. Remove from heat and pour into a small bowl. With a rotary beater, electric mixer or fork, beat vigorously until mixture thickens. Stir in vanilla. Cool before spreading on cake.

Boiled Fruit Cake

2/3 cup cold black tea
1/2 cup butter, cut into
chunks
3/4 cup packed brown sugar
1/2 cup currants
1/2 cup mixed candied peel
1 cup raisins
1 teaspoon apple pie spice
2-1/2 cups all-purpose flour
2 teaspoons baking soda
1 egg, lightly beaten

A quick and easy fruit cake. The rich flavor belies the ease of preparation.

In a medium-size saucepan, combine tea, butter, brown sugar, currants, candied peel, raisins and apple pie spice. Bring to a boil, stirring until sugar is dissolved. Reduce heat; cover and simmer gently 20 minutes. Remove from heat and set aside to cool. Preheat oven to 350F (175C). Grease a round 2-inch-deep, 8-inch-diameter cake pan; set aside. Sift flour and baking soda into a large bowl. Beat in cooled fruit mixture, then egg. Pour into pan. Bake 1 hour or until a wooden pick inserted in center comes out clean. Cool in pan 30 minutes, then turn out onto a wire rack to cool completely. Makes 8 to 10 servings.

Sour Cream Chocolate Cake

1/2 cup unsweetened cocoa
    powder
1/2 cup boiling water
2 cups all-purpose flour
2 teaspoons baking powder
1/2 teaspoon salt
2 tablespoons butter or
    margarine, room
    temperature
1-1/2 cups sugar
2 egg yolks
1 teaspoon vanilla extract
1 teaspoon baking soda
1/2 pint (1 cup) dairy sour
    cream
1/4 cup raspberry jam

Light, tender, chocolaty—this cake is irresistible.

In a small bowl, stir together cocoa powder and boiling water until smooth; set aside to cool. Preheat oven to 375F (190C). Grease 2 round 8-inch cake pans; set aside. Sift flour, baking powder and salt into a medium-size bowl; set aside. In a large bowl, cream butter and sugar until blended. Beat in egg yolks and vanilla. Stir baking soda into sour cream; fold into creamed mixture. Fold in dry ingredients and mix well. Beat in cocoa mixture. Divide between pans; smooth tops. Bake 20 to 25 minutes or until top of cake springs back when lightly touched. Cool in pans a few minutes, then turn out onto wire racks to cool completely. Sandwich layers together with jam. Makes 8 to 10 servings.

Swiss Roll

3/4 cup all-purpose flour
1/2 teaspoon baking powder
3 eggs
1 cup superfine sugar
1 tablespoon water
1/4 cup raspberry jam

Despite its continental name, this version of the jelly roll is a very English teatime treat. If the cake cools too much and becomes difficult to roll easily, dampen a kitchen towel in hot water, wring out and place under the parchment paper. The cake should soften again.

Preheat oven to 400F (205C). Grease a 13" x 9" baking pan; set aside. Sift flour and baking powder into a small bowl; set aside. In a large bowl and using a wire whisk, an electric mixer or a fork, beat together eggs and 1/2 cup superfine sugar until thick and creamy. Fold in dry ingredients, then stir in water. Pour batter into pan, smoothing top. Bake 10 minutes or until top springs back when lightly touched. Meanwhile, lay out a sheet of parchment paper and sprinkle it with remaining 1/2 cup superfine sugar. As soon as cake is done, turn it out onto paper. Trim off crusty edges of cake with a sharp knife. Spread cake with jam. Roll up firmly, starting from a short end. Cool on a wire rack. Makes 8 to 10 servings.

Variation
Chocolate Swiss Roll: Replace 1 tablespoon of the flour with 1 tablespoon unsweetened cocoa powder.

Sometimes plain, sometimes fruited, loaf cakes are an excellent addition to your afternoon tea table. These simple cakes are an especially good choice if you have limited time for preparation on the day of the party since they can be made a day or two ahead of time. Wrap baked cakes snugly in foil, then package airtight and store at room temperature or in the refrigerator until shortly before party time.

Orange Tea Loaf

2 cups self-rising flour
2-1/2 teaspoons baking
   powder
Pinch of salt
1/4 cup butter or margarine,
   room temperature
3/4 cup sugar
1 egg
Grated peel of 1/2 orange
2 tablespoons orange juice
2 tablespoons milk
Butter

This cake tastes even better a day or two after baking.

Preheat oven to 375F (190C). Grease an 8" x 4" loaf pan; set aside. Sift flour, baking powder and salt into a medium-size bowl; set aside. In a large bowl, cream 1/4 cup butter and sugar with an electric mixer or a wooden spoon until light and fluffy. Beat in egg, then orange peel, orange juice and milk. Fold in dry ingredients. Spoon into pan; smooth top. Bake 40 to 50 minutes or until a wooden pick inserted in center comes out clean. Cool in pan 5 minutes, then turn out onto a wire rack to cool completely. Wrap loaf airtight and store 1 or 2 days before serving. Slice and serve with butter. Makes 8 to 10 servings.

Fig Loaf

3 cups all-purpose flour
2 teaspoons baking powder
1/2 teaspoon salt
1 teaspoon ground cinnamon
1 teaspoon ground nutmeg
1/2 teaspoon ground cloves
1/2 cup chopped dried figs
2 cups chopped raisins
1 cup butter or margarine,
   room temperature
2 cups packed brown sugar
4 eggs
1 cup water

Rich, sweetly spiced and studded with figs and raisins.

Preheat oven to 325F (165C). Grease a 9" x 5" loaf pan; set aside. Sift flour, baking powder, salt, cinnamon, nutmeg and cloves into a large bowl. Add figs and raisins and toss lightly to coat with flour; set aside. In another large bowl, cream butter and brown sugar with an electric mixer or a wooden spoon until fluffy. Beat in eggs 1 at a time. Alternately add flour mixture and water, mixing well after each addition. Pour into pan, smoothing top. Bake about 2 hours or until a wooden pick inserted in center comes out clean. Cool in pan 5 minutes, then turn out onto a wire rack to cool completely. To serve, cut loaf in slices. Makes 8 to 10 servings.

On the preceding pages: A potpourri of sweets nearly ready for the tea table: Drunken Plum Tart, page 92; chocolate cupcakes for Chocolate Butterflies, page 121; Shrove Tuesday Pancakes, page 137; Dundee Cake, page 110; and Fruit Tartlets, page 96.

A favorite with hostesses, Orange Tea Loaf is best made a day or two ahead so flavors meld and slicing is easier.

Hazelnut Tea Loaf

3 cups all-purpose flour
2 teaspoons baking powder
3/4 cup butter or margarine,
  room temperature
1-1/2 cups sugar
2 eggs
1 teaspoon vanilla extract
1/2 cup milk
3 tablespoons orange juice
1 tablespoon grated orange
  peel
1 cup hazelnuts, finely
  chopped
1/2 cup hazelnuts, coarsely
  chopped

An elusive touch of orange adds interest to this loaf. Finely chopped hazelnuts are folded into the cake batter; larger pieces make a crunchy topping.

Preheat oven to 350F (175C). Grease a 9" x 5" loaf pan; set aside. Sift flour and baking powder into a medium-size bowl; set aside. In a large bowl, cream butter and sugar with an electric mixer or a wooden spoon until light and fluffy. Beat in eggs 1 at a time. Beat in vanilla. Mix milk and orange juice; beat into creamed mixture alternately with dry ingredients. Stir in orange peel and finely chopped hazelnuts. Pour into pan; smooth top. Sprinkle coarsely chopped hazelnuts on top and press lightly into batter. Bake about 20 minutes or until a wooden pick inserted in center comes out clean. Cool in pan 5 minutes, then turn out onto a wire rack to cool completely. To serve, cut cake in slices. Makes 8 to 10 servings.

Oaty Apple Loaf

1-1/2 cups all-purpose flour
1 teaspoon baking powder
1 teaspoon baking soda
1/2 teaspoon salt
1 teaspoon ground cinnamon
1 teaspoon ground nutmeg
2/3 cup packed light brown
  sugar
1 cup quick-cooking rolled
  oats
1 cup coarsely chopped
  walnuts
2 eggs
1/4 cup milk
1/4 cup butter or margarine,
  melted, cooled
2 medium-size apples, cored,
  coarsely shredded
Butter

Serve this one in winter. It's hearty, fruity, spicy, filling—just the thing for cold days.

Preheat oven to 350F (175C). Lightly grease a 9" x 5" loaf pan; set aside. Sift flour, baking powder, baking soda, salt, cinnamon and nutmeg into a large bowl. Stir in brown sugar, rolled oats and walnuts. In a small bowl, mix eggs, milk and melted butter. Add all at once to dry ingredients. Add apples and stir gently until all ingredients are blended. Pour into pan; smooth top. Bake 50 to 55 minutes or until a wooden pick inserted in center comes out clean. Cool in pan 10 minutes, then turn out onto a wire rack to cool completely. To serve, cut loaf in slices. Serve with butter. Makes 8 to 10 servings.

Hazelnut Meringue

**4 egg whites, room
temperature**
**1 cup plus 2 tablespoons
superfine sugar**
1/2 teaspoon vanilla extract
1/2 teaspoon white vinegar
1 cup ground hazelnuts
**1/2 pint (1 cup) whipping
cream**
**1 pint (2 cups) fresh
raspberries, rinsed**
1 tablespoon powdered sugar

This is the perfect choice for summer tea on the lawn.

Preheat oven to 375F (190C). Grease and lightly flour 2 round 8-inch cake pans. Line pans with 8-inch parchment paper circles; grease and lightly flour parchment. Set aside. In a large bowl, beat egg whites with an electric mixer or whisk until stiff peaks form. Gradually add superfine sugar and continue beating until meringue is very stiff. Beat in vanilla and vinegar. Fold in hazelnuts. Divide between pans, smoothing tops. Bake 30 to 40 minutes or until very pale brown. Cool in pans on a wire rack. To serve, carefully remove layers from pans. Whip cream in a medium-size bowl until stiff. Place 1 meringue on serving plate. Cover with 1/2 of whipped cream. Dot raspberries over cream. Cover with remaining cream. Set remaining meringue on top. Dust with powdered sugar. Serve at once. Makes 8 to 10 servings.

~ Individual Cakes ~

Small cakes are almost always served at teatime. They're especially important at large gatherings where it is difficult to hand around slices of larger cakes. Besides being easier for your guests to handle, small cakes and bars offer you the opportunity for more creativity — you can be a little more elaborate and colorful with your decorations.

Coburg Cakes

6 blanched almonds, halved
1-1/4 cups all-purpose flour
1 teaspoon baking soda
1/2 teaspoon ground allspice
1/2 teaspoon ground ginger
**1/2 teaspoon ground
cinnamon**
**1/4 cup butter or margarine,
room temperature**
1/4 cup superfine sugar
1 egg
**1 tablespoon light corn
syrup**
1/4 cup milk

Serve these little cakes bottom-side-up so the almond is on top.

Preheat oven to 350F (145C). Grease 12 (3-inch) fluted cake pans or muffin cups. Place almond half in bottom of each pan; set aside. Sift flour, baking soda, allspice, ginger and cinnamon into a medium-size bowl. In a large bowl, cream butter and superfine sugar with an electric mixer or a wooden spoon until light and fluffy. Add egg and beat well. In a small bowl, stir together corn syrup and milk. Alternately add dry ingredients and milk mixture to creamed mixture, beating until smooth after each addition. Divide among cake pans. Bake about 25 minutes or until tops spring back when lightly touched. Cool briefly in pans, then turn out onto a wire rack to cool completely. Makes 12 cakes.

Ladyfingers

3 egg whites, room
temperature
6 tablespoons powdered
sugar
2 egg yolks, beaten
1/2 teaspoon vanilla extract
1/3 cup all-purpose flour,
sifted

Oh-so-proper for afternoon tea, ladyfingers are as dainty as they sound.

Preheat oven to 300F (150C). Cover a large baking sheet with parchment paper; *do not* grease paper. Set aside. In a medium-size bowl, beat egg whites until stiff peaks form. Fold in 5 tablespoons powdered sugar. Mix in egg yolks and vanilla. Fold in flour gently but thoroughly. Put batter into a pastry bag fitted with a 1-inch tip. Pipe 4-inch-long fingers of batter onto parchment. Sprinkle batter with remaining 1 tablespoon powdered sugar. Bake about 10 minutes or until light golden brown. Transfer to a wire rack to cool completely. Makes about 8 ladyfingers.

Variation
Sponge Drops: Instead of piping batter from a pastry bag, simply drop teaspoonfuls of mixture onto baking sheet. Bake 8 to 10 minutes. When cool, glaze tops with Honey Icing.

Honey Icing:
1 cup mild honey
2 egg whites, room
temperature

Honey Icing:
In a medium-size saucepan, boil honey about 10 minutes or until quite dark and *very* runny. Remove from heat and set aside to cool. In a medium-size bowl, beat egg whites until they hold very stiff peaks. Pour cooled honey into egg whites in a thin stream, beating constantly until mixture reaches a spreading consistency. Cool completely before using.

Rock Cakes

2 cups all-purpose flour
2 teaspoons baking powder
Pinch of salt
1/2 teaspoon ground nutmeg
1/4 teaspoon ground
cinnamon
1/4 teaspoon ground cloves
1/4 cup cold butter, cut in
small pieces
1/4 cup solid vegetable
shortening, chilled, cut in
pieces
1/3 cup raisins
1/3 cup chopped walnuts
2/3 cup packed light brown
sugar
Grated peel of 1/2 lemon
1 egg, lightly beaten
1 to 2 tablespoons milk

To some English people, the mention of rock cakes brings back memories of school days: these big spicy cakes seem to be a regular item on the tea menu of many boarding schools. When fresh, rock cakes are delicious—but leave them a day or two and they take on all the characteristics of their namesake!

Preheat oven to 400F (205C). Grease a large baking sheet; set aside. Sift flour, baking powder, salt, nutmeg, cinnamon and cloves into a large bowl. With your fingers, rub in butter and shortening until mixture is crumbly. Stir in raisins, walnuts, brown sugar and lemon peel. Add egg and just enough milk to make a stiff dough. Drop tablespoonfuls of dough 2 inches apart on baking sheet. Bake 12 to 15 minutes or until golden brown. Transfer to a wire rack to cool. Serve fresh. Makes about 15 rock cakes.

Eccles Cakes

2 tablespoons butter
1/2 cup packed brown sugar
1/2 cup raisins
1/4 cup currants
1/4 cup chopped mixed
   candied peel
1/2 teaspoon ground allspice
1/4 teaspoon ground nutmeg
1/4 teaspoon ground
   cinnamon
1 recipe Short-Crust Pastry,
   page 86
1 egg white, lightly beaten
1/4 cup granulated sugar

Eccles is a town in Lancashire in the north of England. These little pastries—traditionally called "cakes"—probably originate there.

In a medium-size saucepan, gently warm butter and brown sugar over low heat until butter is melted. Remove from heat. Add raisins, currants, candied peel, allspice, nutmeg and cinnamon and mix thoroughly; set aside to cool. Preheat oven to 425F (220C). Grease a large baking sheet; set aside. On a lightly floured surface, thinly roll out pastry with a floured rolling pin. Cut into rounds with a 4-inch cookie cutter. Divide fruit mixture among pastry rounds, mounding it in centers. Pull edges of pastry up over filling and pinch together in middle to seal. Place cakes seam-side down on baking sheet. Brush with egg white and sprinkle with granulated sugar. Bake about 15 minutes or until pastry is golden brown. Transfer to a wire rack to cool. Makes about 10 cakes.

Chocolate Butterflies

1 cup self-rising flour
1 teaspoon baking powder
3 tablespoons unsweetened
   cocoa powder
1/2 cup butter or margarine,
   room temperature
1/2 cup superfine sugar
2 eggs

Orange Buttercream Topping:
1/2 cup unsalted butter,
   room temperature
2 cups powdered sugar
About 1 tablespoon orange
   juice
1 teaspoon finely grated
   orange peel

These are an attractive variation on cupcakes.

Preheat oven to 375F (190C). Stand 24 paper baking cups in 2-1/2 to 3-inch muffin cups; set aside. Sift flour, baking powder and cocoa into a medium-size bowl; set aside. In a large bowl, cream butter and superfine sugar with an electric mixer or a wooden spoon until light and fluffy. Beat in eggs 1 at a time. Fold in dry ingredients and blend well. Spoon batter into baking cups. Bake 20 minutes or until tops spring back when lightly touched. Place cupcakes on a wire rack to cool completely. Meanwhile, prepare Orange Buttercream Topping; set aside. Slice off rounded tops of cupcakes; cut each rounded piece in half lengthwise and set aside. Spread tops of cakes with a thin layer of buttercream. Spoon remaining buttercream into pastry bag fitted with a small plain tip. Pipe a strip of buttercream down center of each cake. Make "wings" on each cake by arranging 2 reserved half-slices of cake, rounded edges together, at an angle on each side of piped line. Makes 24 cakes.

Orange Buttercream Topping:
In a medium-size bowl, beat butter with an electric mixer or a wooden spoon until creamy. Gradually add powdered sugar and continue beating until light and fluffy. Beat in orange juice and orange peel.

Vienna Tarts

1 cup all-purpose flour
1/4 cup cornstarch
Pinch of salt
1 cup butter, room
    temperature
1/2 cup powdered sugar
1/2 teaspoon vanilla extract
Milk, if needed
About 2 tablespoons
    strawberry jam

Buttery, jam-centered Vienna tarts are particularly rich and crumbly.

~ Preheat oven to 350F (175C). Stand 10 small paper baking cups in 2-inch muffin cups; set aside. Sift flour, cornstarch and salt into a medium-size bowl; set aside. In a large bowl, cream butter and 1/4 cup powdered sugar with an electric mixer or a wooden spoon until smooth. Fold in dry ingredients. Stir in vanilla. Add milk 1 tablespoon at a time until mixture reaches soft piping consistency. Spoon dough into a pastry bag fitted with a 1/2-inch star tip. Pipe dough into paper cups, covering base and working up sides in a spiral. Bake 20 to 25 minutes or until light golden. Cool on a wire rack. Dust cooled pastries with remaining 1/4 cup powdered sugar. Spoon about 1/2 teaspoon strawberry jam in center of each cake. Makes 10 cakes.

Petits Fours

3 eggs
1/2 cup superfine sugar
1-1/2 teaspoons vanilla
    extract
Pinch of salt
2/3 cup all-purpose flour,
    sifted
1/4 cup butter, melted,
    cooled
1 recipe Marzipan,
    page 108
About 1/4 cup strawberry
    jelly
Powdered sugar
Fondant Icing (recipe
    follows)
Silver dragées
Crystallized flower petals
Candied cherries, quartered
Fondant Icing:
1/2 cup plus 2 tablespoons
    water
2 cups superfine sugar
Pinch of cream of tartar
Red, green and yellow food
    coloring

Petits fours, fancies, dainties—call them what you will, they are the delectable mouthfuls that add the color to your tea table.

~ Preheat oven to 350F (175C). Grease an 8-inch-square baking pan; set aside. In a large bowl, beat eggs, superfine sugar, vanilla and salt with an electric mixer until very thick, creamy and pale. (If you don't have a mixer, pour mixture into the top of a double boiler over simmering water, making sure bottom does not touch water. Beat vigorously with a wire whisk or a fork until mixture reaches correct consistency, then remove from heat.) Gently fold in 1/4 of flour, then add 1/3 of melted butter. Repeat until all flour and butter have been mixed in. Pour batter into pan. Bake about 25 minutes or until cake is light golden brown. Cool in pan 5 minutes, then turn out onto a wire rack to cool completely. Meanwhile, prepare Marzipan; set aside. Cut off crisp edges of cake; cut cake into small (about 1-1/2-inch) squares. Spread top and sides of each square with jelly. On a surface dusted with powdered sugar and using a rolling pin covered with powdered sugar, roll out marzipan to a thickness of 1/8 inch. Cut into squares to fit tops of cakes; cut strips to fit around sides. Press marzipan gently in place over cakes, pinching ends and edges together gently to seal. Let stand, uncovered, in a cool, dry place overnight. Before serving, prepare Fondant Icing in an assortment of colors. Coat cakes with icing as directed. Decorate with silver dragées, flower petals and candied cherries. Makes about 20 petits fours.

A rainbow of fondant-coated petits fours conceal a layer of marzipan, which is molded atop the cake squares.

Fondant Icing:

In a medium-size, heavy saucepan, heat water and superfine sugar over low heat, without stirring, until sugar is dissolved. Bring to a boil, shaking pan occasionally. Stir in cream of tartar and boil until syrup reaches a temperature of 240F (120C) on a candy thermometer. Pour into a bowl and cool until a thin crust forms on top. Beat until icing is thickened. Turn out onto a cold surface such as a marble slab, a tiled countertop or a board that has been refrigerated. With a blunt-ended knife, turn icing in a figure 8 pattern until smooth, then knead gently until thick and creamy. Return to bowl. To use, set over a pan of simmering water. Stir gently until icing melts into a creamy liquid. Pour into 3 warm bowls. Add 1 or 2 drops food coloring to each bowl and mix gently. To coat cakes, skewer the bottom of each with a fork and dip into one of the icings. Set right-side-up on a wire rack and decorate while icing is still wet.

Fruits, Mousses & Other Tea Desserts

Ices have been served at teatime since the heyday of tea gardens in the 18th century. Along with fresh fruits and light desserts, they're still served at afternoon tea, especially in summer. Purchased or homemade ice milk, sherbets and sorbets are all good choices, as are chocolate mousse, trifle and the other recipes in this chapter. If you'd like to serve a rich ice cream, keep portions dainty—just one small scoop per serving.

Almond Crème

1 (1/4-oz.) envelope
   unflavored gelatin (about 1
   tablespoon)
3 tablespoons cold water
3 tablespoons boiling water
1/2 cup sugar
2 eggs
1-1/2 cups whipping cream
1/2 teaspoon almond extract
6 blanched almonds, halved
Sliced fresh fruit, if desired

Often inflicted on children at teatime or fed to the sick (much like chicken soup!), traditional English creamy desserts, such as junket and blancmange, tend to be somewhat bland-tasting. A welcome departure from the usual, almond crème is much more sophisticated and flavorful.

In a small bowl, sprinkle gelatin over cold water. Stir; set aside a few minutes to soften. Add boiling water and stir until gelatin is completely dissolved. In a medium-size bowl, stir together sugar, eggs, cream and almond extract. Using a rotary beater or an electric mixer, beat until mixture holds stiff peaks. Add gelatin mixture and continue beating until well blended. Spoon into 6 pretty glasses. Refrigerate about 30 minutes or until set. To serve, decorate each dessert with 2 almond halves and fresh fruit. Makes 6 servings.

Peach Crème Fraîche

1 (1/4-oz.) envelope
   unflavored gelatin (about 1
   tablespoon)
3 tablespoons cold water
3 tablespoons boiling water
3 medium-size peaches,
   peeled, pitted, sliced
Lemon juice
1 (8-oz.) carton (1 cup) plain
   yogurt
1/2 teaspoon almond extract
1/4 cup sugar
6 small mint sprigs

If you prefer, make this dessert in a large dish or mold and turn it out onto a decorative plate to serve.

In a small bowl, sprinkle gelatin over cold water. Stir; set aside a few minutes to soften. Add boiling water and stir until gelatin is completely dissolved; set aside. Reserve 6 peach slices for decoration; brush with lemon juice to prevent darkening, then cover and refrigerate. Put remaining peach slices in a blender or food processor. Add yogurt and almond extract and process until smooth. Add sugar and process until blended. Add gelatin mixture and process 10 seconds longer. Spoon into 6 pretty glasses. Refrigerate about 1 hour or until set. To serve, decorate each dessert with 1 of the reserved peach slices and 1 mint sprig. Makes 6 servings.

On the preceding pages: A romantic tea for two, set up late-afternoon in the shade of the gazebo, features assorted tea sandwiches, pages 48-51, fresh strawberries, Victoria Sandwich Sponge, page 106, and chilled champagne—which is lovely après-tea.

Fresh strawberries and cream . . . . What more need one say? Simply select the largest berries available, arrange them in an elegant crystal bowl, and serve with a scandalous amount of freshly whipped cream. Heaven!

Strawberries & Cream

**1 quart (4 cups) fresh
   strawberries
1/4 cup superfine sugar
1 to 2 cups whipping cream**

What could be simpler or more delicious than fresh strawberries and rich cream? This classic combination is found on every English tea table in summer, and traditionally served in the tea tents at the All-England Lawn Tennis Club during Wimbledon fortnight. Why not have a Wimbledon tea party and serve berries and cream while watching tennis on television?

Wash and hull strawberries; pat dry. Arrange in 6 pretty glass dishes. Sprinkle lightly with superfine sugar. In a large bowl, beat cream until stiff. Top each serving of strawberries with a spoonful of whipped cream. Offer remaining cream at the table so guests can help themselves. (Alternatively, you may serve strawberries, sugar and cream separately.) Makes 6 servings.

Variation
Substitute fresh raspberries for the strawberries.

Sherry Trifle

Egg Custard Sauce (recipe follows)
1 layer Victoria Sponge Cake, page 106, cut in about 1" x 3" strips *or* 1 recipe Ladyfingers (about 8 ladyfingers), page 120
1/2 cup strawberry jam
1/2 cup sweet sherry, preferably Harveys Bristol Cream
1 pint (2 cups) whipping cream
Fresh strawberries
Halved blanched almonds

Egg Custard Sauce:
1 pint (2 cups) whole milk
4 eggs
2 tablespoons sugar
1/2 teaspoon vanilla extract

Trifle makes a very adult addition to a sit-down high tea. Though not exclusively a holiday recipe, it's often served at teatime on Christmas Day or the day after (Boxing Day).

Prepare and chill Egg Custard Sauce. Spread all sides of cake strips or ladyfingers with jam. Arrange in bottom of a pretty glass serving bowl at least 6 inches deep. Slowly pour sherry over cake; tip bowl so cake completely absorbs sherry. Pour cold custard sauce over cake; smooth top. Beat cream in a large bowl until it holds stiff peaks; spread a layer of cream over custard. Spoon remaining cream into a pastry bag fitted with a 1/2-inch star tip; pipe cream in rosettes over trifle. Decorate with strawberries and almonds. Serve shortly after assembling. Makes 10 to 12 servings.

Egg Custard Sauce:
Heat milk in a heavy saucepan over low heat until very hot; do not boil. While milk heats, beat eggs, sugar and vanilla in a large bowl. When milk is hot, pour it in a thin stream into egg mixture, stirring constantly. Mix well, then pour back into saucepan. Stir over medium heat until custard thickens enough to coat the back of a metal spoon. Pour into a clean bowl; cover custard to prevent a skin from forming on surface. Refrigerate until cold.

White Chocolate-Dipped Strawberries

1 pint (2 cups) fresh strawberries, washed, patted dry but not hulled
1/4 cup Grand Marnier
6 ounces white chocolate

For something a little exotic, consider strawberries served this way. You will need a kitchen hypodermic needle, available in many gourmet stores, or a disposable hypodermic from a drugstore.

Use kitchen hypodermic needle to inject about 1/2 teaspoon Grand Marnier into each strawberry. Refrigerate for at least 1 hour. Cover a large baking sheet with waxed paper. Melt white chocolate in the top of a double boiler over hot but not boiling water. Holding strawberries by the stems, dip about 2/3 of each berry into chocolate. Let excess chocolate drip off, then set strawberry on baking sheet. When all strawberries have been dipped, place baking sheet in refrigerator for about 1/2 hour or until chocolate is solid. Serve chilled. Serves 8.

Sherry-laced cake, fruit, custard sauce and whipped cream layered into a glass bowl become glamorous trifle.

Pavlova

3 egg whites, room
    temperature
Pinch of salt
3/4 cup superfine sugar
1/4 cup granulated sugar
1 tablespoon cornstarch
1 teaspoon lemon juice
1 pint (2 cups) whipping
    cream
Fresh fruit to decorate, such
    as strawberries,
    raspberries, sliced peaches
    and/or sliced kiwifruit

A wonderful centerpiece for your tea party, this impressive dessert comes from Australia (where afternoon tea is as much of an institution as it is in England). Pavlova was created in honor of the famous ballerina when she visited "down under." The meringue should be crisp on the outside, but soft and marshmallow-like inside.

Preheat oven to 210F (100C). Cover 2 baking sheets with foil. Using plates or empty cake pans as guides, mark a 7-inch circle on 1 baking sheet and a 5-inch circle on the other; set aside. In a large bowl, beat egg whites with salt until stiff peaks form. Gradually add superfine sugar, beating constantly until very stiff and glossy. Combine granulated sugar and cornstarch and gently fold into meringue. Gently stir in lemon juice. With a knife, spread a layer of meringue about 1/4 inch thick onto each marked circle on foil. Spoon remaining meringue into a pastry bag fitted with a 1-inch star tip. Pipe swirls of meringue around edge of each circle to form a shell. Bake 30 minutes. Turn off oven but do not remove meringue shells until oven has cooled completely, about 1 to 1-1/2 hours. Shortly before serving, beat cream in a large bowl until it holds stiff peaks. Place larger meringue shell on a serving plate. Spread center generously with whipped cream. Place smaller shell on top and fill center with remaining whipped cream. Decorate with fruit. Serve at once. Makes 10 to 12 servings.

Syllabub

3/4 cup whipping cream
2 egg whites, room
    temperature
1/2 cup superfine sugar
Juice of 1/2 lemon (about 2
    tablespoons)
6 tablespoons sweet white
    wine
2 tablespoons brandy
Candied citron
Ground nutmeg

This old English delicacy was traditionally made with milk warm from the cow, poured from a height over wine, brandy, cider or ale. The resulting frothy mixture was sweetened and flavored with spices. Today, making an authentic syllabub may be a little impractical for most of us! Here's a version you can easily handle in your kitchen.

In a small bowl, beat cream until it holds stiff peaks; set aside. In a large bowl, beat egg whites until they hold stiff peaks. Fold in superfine sugar, lemon juice, wine, brandy and whipped cream. Divide mixture among 6 pretty glasses or sherbet dishes. Refrigerate several hours before serving. To serve, decorate with citron and sprinkle with nutmeg. Makes 6 small servings.

Rich yet light and velvety smooth, chocolate leaf-and-whipped cream-topped Chocolate Mousse truly pleasures the tastebuds.

Chocolate Mousse

1-1/2 teaspoons unflavored gelatin
1-1/2 tablespoons cold water
3 tablespoons boiling water
3/4 cup sugar
2/3 cup unsweetened cocoa powder
1-1/2 cups whipping cream
1-1/2 teaspoons vanilla extract
6 chocolate leaves or 18 fresh raspberries
Whipped cream

A light dessert, perfect for a summer high tea.

In a small bowl, sprinkle gelatin over cold water. Stir; set aside a few minutes to soften. Add boiling water and stir until gelatin is completely dissolved. In a medium-size bowl, stir together sugar and cocoa. Add cream and vanilla. Using a rotary beater or an electric mixer, beat until mixture holds stiff peaks. Add gelatin mixture and continue beating until well blended. Spoon into 6 pretty glasses. Refrigerate about 30 minutes or until set. To serve, decorate each dessert with a chocolate leaf or 3 raspberries and whipped cream. Makes 6 servings.

Recipes for Holidays & Special Occasions

Practically every milestone in life, from christenings to wakes, is celebrated with tea parties in Britain! And almost every month of the year offers the opportunity to cook up special dishes to celebrate holidays or other special days. Here are some traditional and seasonal recipes that can make an afternoon tea a real event.

Valentine Kisses sandwiched together with whipped cream is a sweet offering any time of the year, especially on February 14th.

Valentine Kisses

2 egg whites, room temperature
2/3 cup superfine sugar
1 drop red food coloring
1/3 cup whipping cream

What better excuse than Valentine's Day to have romantic tea for two?

Preheat oven to 250F (120C). Cover a large baking sheet with parchment paper; coat lightly with nonstick cooking spray. Set aside. In a large bowl, beat egg whites until they hold stiff peaks. Gradually add superfine sugar and beat until mixture is very stiff and glossy. Put 1/2 of mixture into another bowl. Add food coloring to 1 bowl and mix carefully. With a teaspoon or pastry bag fitted with a small star tip, make small mounds of meringue 2 inches apart on baking sheet. Bake about 1-1/4 hours or until meringues are dry and crisp. Cool on baking sheet. To serve, beat cream in a small deep bowl until it holds stiff peaks. Sandwich cooled meringues together with cream, using 1 white and 1 pink meringue for each "sandwich." Makes about 20 kisses.

On the preceding pages: A holiday buffet tea welcomes friends and relatives who come to call. Sausage Rolls, page 45, Yule Log and Christmas Mince Pies, both on page 140, are traditions which are bound to be part of almost everyone's menu.

Simnel Cake

1 recipe Marzipan,
   page 108
2 cups all-purpose flour
1/2 teaspoon salt
1/2 teaspoon ground
   cinnamon
1/4 teaspoon ground nutmeg
1/4 teaspoon ground allspice
1-1/3 cups currants
2/3 cup raisins
1/2 cup chopped mixed
   candied peel
1/2 cup candied cherries,
   quartered
2/3 cup butter, room
   temperature
3/4 cup granulated sugar
3 eggs
Powdered sugar
1 egg white

This spicy fruitcake was once traditionally eaten on Mothering Sunday, which is the first Sunday in May. Today, though, it's more closely associated with Easter—so this version of Simnel cake is decorated with nearly a dozen marzipan "eggs."

Prepare Marzipan; set aside. Preheat oven to 300F (150C). Grease a round 2-inch-deep, 9-inch-diameter cake pan. Line pan with parchment paper; grease paper. Set aside. Sift flour, salt, cinnamon, nutmeg and allspice into a medium-size bowl. Stir in currants, raisins, candied peel and candied cherries; set aside. In a large bowl, beat butter and granulated sugar with an electric mixer or a wooden spoon until light and fluffy. Beat in eggs 1 at a time. Fold in dry ingredients. Spoon 1/2 of batter into cake pan; set aside. On a surface dusted with powdered sugar and using a rolling pin covered with powdered sugar, roll out 1/3 of marzipan to make a circle 8 inches in diameter. Place atop batter in pan. Carefully spoon remaining batter over marzipan; smooth top. Bake 2-1/2 to 3 hours or until cake is firm to the touch. Cool in pan about 30 minutes, then turn out onto a wire rack to cool completely. Leave cake on rack until decorated. Divide remaining marzipan in half. Roll out 1 portion into a circle to fit top of cake. Lightly beat egg white and brush over top of cake. Set marzipan circle on top. With your hands, form remaining marzipan into 10 "eggs" and arrange around top edge of cake. Brush top and "eggs" with egg white. Preheat broiler. With cake still on wire rack, set on baking sheet and broil 3 inches from heat source 1 to 2 minutes or until marzipan is very lightly browned. Cool before serving. Makes 8 to 10 servings.

Easter Cookies

3 cups all-purpose flour
1/2 teaspoon salt
1/2 teaspoon apple pie spice
1-1/2 cups butter, room
   temperature
1 cup granulated sugar
1 egg
1/2 cup currants
1/2 cup chopped mixed
   candied peel
1 tablespoon superfine sugar

For an attractive presentation, serve these rich cookies in halves of a large, hollow decorative Easter egg.

Preheat oven to 350F (175C). Grease a large baking sheet; set aside. Sift flour, salt and apple pie spice into a large bowl. Set aside. In another large bowl, cream butter and granulated sugar with an electric mixer or a wooden spoon until light and fluffy. Beat in egg. Alternately add dry ingredients, currants and candied peel to make a soft dough. Turn out onto a lightly floured surface. With a floured rolling pin, roll out dough to a thickness of 1/8 inch. Cut in rounds with a 3-inch cookie cutter. Place on greased baking sheet and sprinkle with superfine sugar. Bake about 10 minutes or until light golden brown. Transfer to a wire rack to cool. Makes about 30 cookies.

Harvest Loaf

4 cups all-purpose flour
1 (1/4-oz.) package active dry
  yeast
1 cup warm water (110F,
  45C)
2 teaspoons salt
1 tablespoon solid vegetable
  shortening
1 egg
Butter
Jam or honey

Harvest festivals are held in country districts in England in autumn. This attractive loaf represents a bountiful wheat harvest. It could just as easily be served at a Thanksgiving tea.

In a large bowl, combine 1/2 cup flour, yeast and water; mix well. Let stand in a warm place about 20 minutes or until mixture is frothy. Sift remaining 3-1/2 cups flour and salt into another large bowl. With your fingers, rub in shortening until mixture is crumbly. Add yeast mixture and stir to make a soft dough. Turn out onto a lightly floured surface and knead about 10 minutes or until dough is smooth and elastic. Place in a greased bowl; turn over to grease top. Cover and let rise in a warm place about 1-1/2 hours or until dough is doubled in bulk. Lightly grease a large baking sheet and dust with flour; set aside. Punch down dough; turn out onto floured surface and knead briefly to release air. Divide dough in 3 equal pieces; with your hands, roll each into a rope about 2 feet long. Join ropes together at 1 end and place on prepared baking sheet. Loosely braid ropes and tuck ends under smoothly. Cover and let rise in a warm place 30 minutes or until puffy. Preheat oven to 450F (230C). Lightly beat egg and brush over top of dough. Bake 30 to 40 minutes or until loaf gives a hollow sound when top is thumped. Serve warm with butter and jam or honey. Makes 8 to 10 servings.

Parkin

2 cups all-purpose flour
1/2 teaspoon salt
1 teaspoon ground ginger
1 teaspoon apple pie spice
1/2 teaspoon ground
  cinnamon
1-1/3 cups regular rolled oats
2/3 cup butter or margarine
2/3 cup packed light brown
  sugar
1/3 cup light corn syrup
1/3 cup dark molasses
1 egg, beaten
2/3 cup milk

Should you have the urge to hold a "Guy Fawkes" tea party, this gingery cake from Yorkshire is the one to make. Guy Fawkes was a 17th-century traitor who tried—unsuccessfully—to blow up the Houses of Parliament. To commemorate his demise, bonfires are lit annually on November 5th in the streets or on common ground, and children burn Guy in effigy. This is also the time of year for fireworks in England.

For best flavor, bake parkin a day ahead of time.

Preheat oven to 325F (165C). Grease a 9-inch-square baking pan. Line with parchment paper; grease paper. Set aside. Sift flour, salt, ginger, apple pie spice and cinnamon into a large bowl; stir in rolled oats. Set aside. In a medium-size saucepan, heat butter, brown sugar, corn syrup and molasses over low heat, stirring until butter is melted and sugar is dissolved. Make a well in center of dry ingredients and pour in molasses mixture. Add egg and milk and mix thoroughly. Pour into cake pan. Bake about 1-1/2 hours or until a wooden pick inserted in center comes out clean. Cool in pan 15 minutes, then turn out onto a wire rack to cool completely. Store cooled cake overnight in an airtight container. To serve, cut in 2-1/4"x2-1/4" squares. Makes 16 squares.

Liberal amounts of superfine sugar and lemon juice top crepe-like Shrove Tuesday Pancakes, which are rolled into cylinders.

Shrove Tuesday Pancakes

1 cup all-purpose flour
Pinch of salt
1 egg
1-1/4 cups milk
1 teaspoon vegetable oil
**About 1/2 cup superfine
     sugar**
2 lemons, halved

Shrove Tuesday is celebrated around the world in various ways, the best known of which is Mardi Gras. The English are a little more sedate—all we do is eat pancakes for tea! These pancakes are more like crêpes than tradition-al American breakfast pancakes. Serve them at an informal tea, and let the guests flip their own.

Sift flour and salt into a medium-size bowl. Beat in egg and 1/2 of milk until batter is smooth. Stir in remaining milk and oil. Transfer to a pitcher for easier pouring. Warm a plate for serving. Preheat a 10-inch crêpe pan or skillet over medium-high heat; grease lightly. Pour a little batter into center of pan, making an area of batter about 3 inches in diameter. Quickly tilt pan in all directions to cover bottom in a thin layer. Cook about 1 minute or until underside of pancake is golden brown (check by lifting edge with a spatula). Turn and cook other side about 30 seconds. Slide pancake onto warm plate. Immediately sprin-kle with about 1 teaspoon superfine sugar and a squeeze of lemon juice. Roll up and keep warm. Repeat with remaining batter, regreasing pan as necessary. Before serving, sprinkle tops of pancakes with remaining sugar and another squeeze of lemon juice. Makes about 12 pancakes.

Hot Cross Buns

4 cups all-purpose flour
1 (1/4-oz.) package active dry
    yeast
1 teaspoon superfine sugar
2/3 cup warm milk (110F,
    45C)
1/4 cup warm water (110F,
    45C)
1 teaspoon salt
1/2 teaspoon apple pie spice
1/2 teaspoon ground
    cinnamon
1/2 teaspoon ground nutmeg
1/4 cup granulated sugar
1/4 cup butter, melted,
    cooled
1 egg
1/2 cup currants
1/2 cup raisins
Glaze (recipe follows)
Butter

Glaze:
2 tablespoons milk
2 tablespoons water
3 tablespoons superfine
    sugar

Hot cross buns are eaten on only one day a year—Good Friday. The symbol marked on top of each bun represents the cross on which Christ died.

In a large bowl, combine 1/2 cup flour, yeast and superfine sugar. Add milk and water and mix well. Let stand in a warm place about 20 minutes or until mixture is frothy. Sift remaining 3-1/2 cups flour, salt, apple pie spice, cinnamon and nutmeg into another large bowl; stir in granulated sugar. Beat melted butter and egg into yeast mixture. Add dry ingredients, currants and raisins and mix to form a soft dough. Turn out onto a lightly floured surface and knead about 10 minutes or until dough is smooth and elastic. Place in a greased bowl; turn over to grease top. Cover and let rise in a warm place about 1-1/2 hours or until doubled in bulk. Dust a large baking sheet with flour; set aside. Punch down dough; turn out onto floured surface and knead well to release air. Divide dough in 12 equal portions. Shape each into a ball and place on baking sheet. Cover and let rise in a warm place 30 minutes or until puffy. Preheat oven to 375F (190C). With a sharp knife, lightly score a cross on top of each bun. Bake about 20 minutes or until golden brown. Meanwhile, prepare Glaze. While buns are still warm, brush twice with Glaze. Transfer to a wire rack to cool. Serve fresh or, if made a day ahead, split and toast. Serve with butter. Makes 12 buns.

Glaze:
In a small saucepan, stir milk, water and superfine sugar over medium heat until sugar is dissolved.

Variation
Make the crosses with strips of pastry or marzipan leftover from other recipes. Place crosses on buns after second rising, just before baking.

Passover Banana Cake

3/4 cup matzo cake meal
1/4 cup potato starch
1/2 teaspoon salt
7 eggs, separated
1 cup sugar
1 cup mashed ripe bananas
Juice of 1/2 lemon (about 2
    tablespoons)
Grated peel of 1/2 lemon
1 cup unsalted mixed nuts,
    chopped

Mashed bananas make this traditional cake moist.

Preheat oven to 350F (175C). Rinse a 9-inch tube pan with water; shake off excess water, but do not dry pan. Set aside. Sift cake meal, potato starch and salt into a small bowl; set aside. In a large bowl, beat egg yolks; gradually add 1/2 cup sugar and continue to beat until light and creamy. Beat in bananas. In another large bowl, beat egg whites until they hold stiff peaks; gradually add remaining 1/2 cup sugar and continue to beat until stiff and shiny. Fold egg yolk mixture into whites. Fold in dry ingredients, then mix in lemon juice, lemon peel and nuts. Pour into pan and bake about 1 hour or until top springs back when lightly touched. Cool in pan on a wire rack. Makes 8 to 10 servings.

Peach jam is spooned into small hollows in the center of chopped walnut-and-cinnamon-spiced Passover Cookies.

Passover Cookies

2 cups matzo cake meal
1/2 teaspoon salt
1/2 teaspoon ground
  cinnamon
2 eggs
1 cup sugar
1 cup peanut oil
1 teaspoon lemon juice
1/4 cup chopped walnuts
About 3 tablespoons peach
  jam

The most observed and celebrated of the Jewish holidays, Passover is an ideal time for a tea. The matzo cake meal is used in place of flour, which is not permitted at Passover.

Preheat oven to 350F (175C). Lightly oil a large baking sheet; set aside. Sift cake meal, salt and cinnamon into a medium-size bowl; set aside. In a large bowl, beat together eggs and sugar. Alternately add oil and dry ingredients, beating well after each addition. Stir in lemon juice and nuts (dough will be soft). With your fingers, pinch off pieces of dough and roll into walnut-size balls. Place balls 2 inches apart on oiled baking sheet and flatten with your hand. With your knuckle, make an indentation in center of each cookie and fill with about 1/4 teaspoon jam. Bake 15 to 20 minutes or until light golden. Transfer to a wire rack to cool. Makes about 36 cookies.

Yule Log

1 Chocolate Swiss Roll,
  page 113
2 ounces semisweet
  chocolate
3 tablespoons granulated
  sugar
1 tablespoon water
1 egg white, room
  temperature
1/2 cup powdered sugar
1-1/2 teaspoons vanilla
  extract
Holly sprig

If traditional Christmas cake is too rich for your taste, try this simpler but still festive recipe. It's also terrific for the children at your Christmas tea party.

Prepare and roll Chocolate Swiss Roll as directed; set aside. In a medium-size saucepan, combine chocolate, granulated sugar and water; stir over low heat until mixture is smooth and glossy and sugar is dissolved. In a medium-size bowl, lightly beat egg white; fold in powdered sugar and stir until smooth. Add chocolate mixture and vanilla and stir well. Cut off small piece from 1 end of cake at an angle. Set large cake on platter. Coat with most of chocolate frosting and swirl with a knife to make a log-like pattern. Arrange cake piece so it juts out from side of "log." Cover with remaining frosting. Decorate with a holly sprig. Makes 8 to 10 servings.

Christmas Mince Pies

1-1/2 recipes Rich
  Short-Crust Pastry, page
  86 (3 cups pastry)
2 cups Bill's Bulk
  Mincemeat, page 140, or
  purchased mincemeat
About 2 tablespoons
  superfine sugar

To the English, Christmas just wouldn't be Christmas without mince pies! They're often served on Christmas Eve at teatime, after midnight mass and again for tea on Boxing Day (the day after Christmas). On Christmas Day, everyone's too stuffed with other goodies to eat them!

Preheat oven to 400F (205C). Grease 10 (2-inch) muffin cups. On a lightly floured surface, thinly roll out 2/3 of pastry with a floured rolling pin. Cut in 10 rounds with a 3-inch cookie cutter. Line muffin cups with pastry. Fill each pastry 2/3 full with mincemeat. Thinly roll out remaining 1/3 of pastry; cut in 10 rounds with a 2-1/2-inch cookie cutter. Set these atop mincemeat as "lids," using a little water to seal the edges. Make a small slit in top of each pie with a sharp knife. Sprinkle pies with superfine sugar. Bake about 20 minutes or until golden brown. Carefully remove from pans and transfer to a wire rack. Serve warm or cold. Makes 10 pies.

Grown-ups and children delight in the festive Yule Log, served as a holiday alternative to fruit- and nut-filled Christmas cakes.

Christmas Cake

2-1/2 cups all-purpose flour
1/2 teaspoon baking powder
1/2 teaspoon salt
1/2 teaspoon ground nutmeg
1/2 teaspoon ground
    cinnamon
2 cups golden raisins
2 cups dark raisins
2 cups currants
1 cup candied cherries,
    chopped
1/2 cup chopped mixed
    candied peel
1 cup blanched almonds,
    chopped
1 cup butter, room
    temperature
1 cup packed light brown
    sugar
4 eggs
Juice of 1 lemon (about 1/4
    cup)
Grated peel of 1 lemon
1 tablespoon molasses
3 tablespoons brandy or dark
    rum
Milk, if needed
1 recipe Marzipan,
    page 108
1/4 cup seedless jam or jelly
    such as plum or grape
Powdered sugar
Small Christmas ornaments
    (for decoration)

Royal Icing:
3 egg whites, room
    temperature
6 cups powdered sugar
2 tablespoons lemon juice

The Christmas feast is usually eaten at midday in England. Even after all that turkey and plum pudding, everyone is still ready to enjoy a slice of rich Christmas cake with friends a few hours later, at teatime. Along with Christmas Mince Pies, Christmas Cake is also served on Boxing Day, when friends you didn't get to see on Christmas Day come for tea.

Preheat oven to 300F (150C). Grease a 9-inch springform pan. Line with a double thickness of parchment paper; grease paper. Set aside. Sift flour, baking powder, salt, nutmeg and cinnamon into a large bowl. Add raisins, currants, candied cherries and candied peel; toss until fruits are well coated with flour. Add almonds; set aside. In another large bowl, beat butter and brown sugar with an electric mixer or a wooden spoon until light and fluffy. Beat in eggs 1 at a time, beating well after each addition. Gradually fold in fruit mixture. Add lemon juice, lemon peel, molasses and brandy. Mix to make a batter that is soft enough to drop from a spoon but too thick to pour; if batter is too stiff, add milk 1 tablespoon at a time. Spoon into baking pan; smooth top. Bake 1 hour. Reduce oven temperature to 275F (135C) and continue to bake 3 to 3-1/2 hours longer or until a wooden pick inserted in center comes out clean. Meanwhile, prepare Marzipan; set aside. Cool cake in pan on a wire rack. When cold, turn out of pan and peel off paper. Spread top and sides thinly with jam. Divide marzipan in half. On a surface dusted with powdered sugar and using a rolling pin covered with powdered sugar, roll out 1 portion to make a circle 9 inches in diameter. Place on top of cake and press gently. Roll out remaining marzipan in a strip as wide as cake is tall and long enough to go around sides of cake; press gently into place. Let cake stand, uncovered, in a cool, dry place 2 to 3 days. Shortly before serving, prepare Royal Icing. Use about 1/2 of icing to coat top and sides of cake. Working out from center of cake and using a straight-sided knife or spatula, spread icing evenly over top and sides of cake. Set cake aside until icing is set. Beat remaining icing until it holds stiff peaks. Spoon icing into a pastry bag fitted with a decorating tip; pipe over cake. Decorate with small Christmas ornaments. Makes 10 to 12 servings.

Royal Icing:
In a large bowl, beat egg whites until frothy. Gradually add powdered sugar and beat until icing holds soft peaks. Quickly beat in lemon juice. (If your kitchen is hot, Royal Icing may start to harden as you are working with it. To prevent this, dampen a kitchen towel in cold water, wring out and drape over bowl.)

Gingerbread Men

2 cups all-purpose flour
1/2 teaspoon baking soda
1/2 teaspoon salt
1/2 teaspoon ground ginger
1/2 teaspoon ground
    cinnamon
1/2 teaspoon ground cloves
1/2 cup molasses
1/4 cup sugar
3 tablespoons solid vegetable
    shortening
1 tablespoon milk

A Christmas treat for the child in all of us. You can also cut this spicy dough into bells, stars, stockings and snowmen. Look for a set of cookie cutters with these seasonal shapes.

Sift flour, baking soda, salt, ginger, cinnamon and cloves into a medium-size bowl; set aside. In a small saucepan, bring molasses to a boil; add sugar, shortening and milk and stir until shortening is melted. Make a well in center of dry ingredients. Pour in molasses mixture and stir to make a soft dough. Cover and refrigerate 1 hour. Preheat oven to 375F (190C). Grease a large baking sheet; set aside. Turn out dough onto a lightly floured surface. With a floured rolling pin, roll out to a thickness of about 1/8 inch. Cut out cookies and place on baking sheet. Bake 8 to 10 minutes or until deep brown. Makes about 15 gingerbread men or 20 smaller cookies.

Hogmanay Black Bun

1 recipe Short-Crust Pastry,
    page 86
2 cups all-purpose flour
1 teaspoon baking soda
1 teaspoon cream of tartar
1 teaspoon ground cinnamon
1 teaspoon ground ginger
1 teaspoon apple pie spice
2-1/2 cups golden raisins
2-1/2 cups currants
1/2 cup chopped mixed
    candied peel
1 cup coarsely chopped
    almonds
2/3 cup packed light brown
    sugar
2 eggs
1/2 cup Scotch whisky
1/4 cup milk

Hogmanay is the Scots name for New Year's Eve. This traditional cake should be made at least 1 week—and as much as 1 month—before serving to give it time to mature.

Preheat oven to 350F (175C). Grease a round 2-inch-deep, 8-inch-diameter baking pan. On a lightly floured surface, thinly roll out 2/3 of pastry with a floured rolling pin to make a round about 14 inches in diameter. Line baking pan with pastry, making sure pastry comes well above pan rim; set aside. Sift flour, baking soda, cream of tartar, cinnamon, ginger and apple pie spice into a large bowl. Mix in raisins, currants, candied peel, almonds and brown sugar. In a small bowl, lightly beat 1 egg with whisky and milk. Add to fruit mixture and stir until evenly moist. Turn into pastry shell; smooth top. Fold edges of pastry over batter. Roll out remaining pastry to make a round 8 inches in diameter. Moisten edges; set pastry atop cake batter and seal edges firmly. With a metal skewer, poke 5 or 6 holes through pastry right down to bottom of cake; prick top with a fork. Beat remaining egg and brush over pastry. Bake 2-1/2 hours, watching to make sure pastry doesn't get too brown; if necessary, lightly cover with foil or brown paper. Cool in pan on a wire rack. Remove from pan. Wrap and store airtight. Serve in very small portions. Makes 12 to 16 servings.

Guilt-Free Afternoon Tea

Let's face it—most of the foods eaten for afternoon tea are on the sweet and rich side. But there's no need to forego afternoon tea if you are concerned with watching your weight. Here are a few recipes that won't cause you to bust your calorie budget.

145

Featherweight Chocolate Chip Cookies

2 egg whites, room
  temperature
2/3 cup superfine sugar
1 teaspoon vanilla extract
Pinch of salt
1 (6-oz.) package (1 cup)
  semisweet chocolate pieces
1/2 cup chopped walnuts

Regular chocolate chip cookies can have as many as 200 calories apiece; these meringue-based drops provide just 45 calories each.

Preheat oven to 350F (175C). Cover a large baking sheet with foil; set aside. In a medium-size bowl, beat egg whites until foamy. Gradually add superfine sugar and beat until stiff peaks form. Mix in vanilla and salt, then fold in chocolate pieces and walnuts. Drop by teaspoonfuls 2 inches apart on baking sheet. Put in oven, then turn off heat and leave cookies at least 5 hours without opening door (they can be left overnight for convenience). Cookies will be a very light brown in color. Store airtight until ready to serve. Makes about 45 cookies.

Skinny Scones

1-1/3 cups wheat flakes (with
  no sugar or salt added)
2/3 cup self-rising flour
1/4 cup raisins
2 tablespoons packed brown
  sugar
1/2 cup nonfat milk
2 tablespoons margarine,
  melted, cooled

These light scones have only about 45 calories each. Eat them fresh from the oven, and pass up the butter!

Preheat oven to 400F (205C). Coat a medium-size baking sheet with nonstick cooking spray; set aside. In a medium-size bowl, combine cereal, flour, raisins and brown sugar. Add milk and melted margarine and mix thoroughly with a wooden spoon. Drop by heaping tablespoonfuls onto baking sheet, spacing about 2 inches apart. Bake 10 to 12 minutes or until golden brown. Serve warm. Makes about 10 scones.

On the preceding pages: A quiet tea for one has great restorative value. Select a cozy corner and indulge yourself with tasty Scotch Oatmeal Cookies, page 80, Featherweight Chocolate Chip Cookies, above—and a single long-stemmed rose.

You can eat almost the entire tray of calorie-controlled Featherweight Chocolate Chip Cookies and not feel (too) guilty.

Banana Tea Bread

1/2 cup frozen unsweetened
   apple juice concentrate,
   thawed
1/2 cup raisins
2-1/2 cups whole-wheat flour
1 tablespoon baking powder
1/4 teaspoon baking soda
1/2 teaspoon ground
   cinnamon
1/4 cup bran flakes
3 medium-size ripe bananas,
   mashed
2/3 cup buttermilk
2 teaspoons vanilla extract
3 egg whites, room
   temperature

This hearty, fat-free, sugar-free tea bread has about 80 calories per slice.

In a small saucepan, heat thawed apple juice concentrate until lukewarm. Remove from heat, add raisins and let soak 15 minutes. Preheat oven to 375F (190C). Coat a 9" x 5" loaf pan with nonstick cooking spray; set aside. In a large bowl, stir together flour, baking powder, baking soda, cinnamon and bran flakes. In another large bowl, stir together bananas, buttermilk, vanilla and apple juice mixture. Add dry ingredients and stir just until mixed. In a medium-size bowl, beat egg whites until stiff peaks form. Gently fold into banana mixture. Spoon into pan. Put in oven, reduce oven temperature to 350F (175C) and bake about 1 hour or until a wooden pick inserted in center comes out clean. Cool in pan 5 minutes, then turn out onto a wire rack to cool completely. To serve, cut loaf in about 1/2-inch-thick slices. Makes about 20 slices.

Sponge Layer Cake

4 eggs
1/2 cup superfine sugar
1 cup all-purpose flour,
   sifted
1/4 cup sugarless fruit
   preserves

Sandwich this cake together with sugarless fruit preserves. A number of excellent brands are sold in health and gourmet food stores. They're usually sweetened with apple or other natural fruit juices and are much lower in calories than traditional jams or jellies.

Preheat oven to 400F (205C). Coat 2 round 8-inch cake pans with nonstick cooking spray; set aside. In a large bowl, beat eggs and super-fine sugar until thick and creamy. Fold in flour. Divide batter between pans. Bake about 20 minutes or until top of cake springs back when lightly touched. Cool layers in pans a few minutes, then turn out onto wire racks to cool completely. Sandwich layers together with preserves. Makes about 8 servings.

Fresh strawberries, lightly steamed with mint to impart a subtle flavor, is the calorie-moderated version of strawberries and cream.

Minted Fresh Strawberries

1 large bunch fresh mint, washed, drained
1 quart (4 cups) fresh strawberries
Juice of 1/2 lemon (about 2 tablespoons)

Though strawberries and cream are traditional summer fare, you can cut out 80 percent of the calories by serving your strawberries with fresh mint instead of cream. The flavor is equally delicious!

Line the basket of a steamer with mint. Wash and hull strawberries. Place them atop mint; cover and steam gently about 10 minutes. Serve sprinkled with a little lemon juice. Makes 8 servings.

Jams & Preserves

There is, of course, a plethora of commercial jams and jellies available. But what could be more delicious than homemade preserves, rich with fruit, to accompany your homemade scones and muffins? These jams and preserves give instant cachet to your tea party, and they're easy and inexpensive to make when you use seasonal fruits. Besides providing you with a year-round supply of instantly available tea-party fare, they also make splendid take-home gifts for your guests.

Amber Marmalade

2 grapefruits
2 thin-skinned oranges
3 lemons
About 3 quarts (12 cups)
    water
6 pounds (12 cups) sugar

Marmalade, used in two recipes in this book, is of course best known as a spread for hot buttered toast, muffins or crumpets. The fruit for this recipe should total about 3 pounds; weigh it in the grocery store when you buy it. The setting point for marmalade is 221F (105C). Test with a candy thermometer, or place a teaspoonful of marmalade on a cold plate and allow to cool for a moment, then push with a fingertip. If the marmalade has reached the proper point, it should wrinkle.

If, despite the lengthy cooking, the peel in your marmalade seems tough, try this technique for the next batch: slice the fruit as directed, then soak in the water overnight before cooking.

Wash and dry fruit. Using a very sharp knife or a food processor with a thin-slicing blade, slice all fruit thinly. Pick out seeds and tie them in a muslin or cheesecloth bag. Put bag and all fruits in a large saucepan; add water (it should cover fruit) and bring to a boil. Cook until peels are tender—usually 1 to 1 1/2 hours, depending on quality and thickness of peel. Remove from heat. Lift out bag of seeds and squeeze liquid back into pan. Add sugar and stir until dissolved. Return to heat and bring to a boil. Boil rapidly until marmalade registers 221F (105C) on a candy thermometer (or test for setting point as described in recipe introduction). Set aside to cool 15 minutes. Pour into hot sterilized 1/2-pint canning jars, leaving about 1/8 inch headspace. Run a narrow spatula down between marmalade and side of jar to release air. Top with sterilized lids; firmly screw on bands. Place in a draft-free area to cool. Store in a cool, dry place. Makes about 7 to 8 pints.

On the preceding pages: The ambience of an informal tea promises to be comforting and companionable. Welsh Batch Scone, page 70, *and Scotch Eggs,* page 43, *served with colorful tomato wedges, are satisfying selections, and everyone will be eager to sample the spreads—Lemon Curd,* page 155, *Amber Marmalade,* above, *and Strawberry Conserve,* page 156.

On the right, the makings for Amber Marmalade—grapefruit, oranges and lemons—are sliced and readied for cooking.

Bill's Bulk Mincemeat

1 pound beef suet, finely
   minced
1 cup brandy
1 quart (4 cups) apple cider
3 cups sugar
2 pounds lean ground beef
4 large apples, peeled, cored,
   diced
2 (16-oz.) cans tart red
   cherries
3 (10-oz.) packages currants
2 (3-1/2-oz.) packages
   candied citron, chopped
1 (24-oz.) package raisins
3 (6-oz.) packages dried
   apricots, finely diced
2 cups chopped walnuts or
   pecans
1 tablespoon ground
   cinnamon
1 tablespoon ground cloves
1 tablespoon ground nutmeg
1 tablespoon ground mace
1 teaspoon salt
1 teaspoon pepper
1 teaspoon ground coriander
1 teaspoon grated lemon peel

This fine recipe lets you make mincemeat from scratch to use in Christmas Mince Pies, page 140. It keeps for a year if properly sealed, and in fact improves with age.

In a medium-size bowl, mix suet with brandy; set aside. In a large saucepan, combine cider and sugar; stir over low heat until sugar is dissolved. Remove from heat. Crumble in beef, then stir in apples, undrained cherries, currants, citron, raisins, apricots, nuts, cinnamon, cloves, nutmeg, mace, salt, pepper, coriander and lemon peel; mix well. Add suet and brandy and mix well. Return to heat and bring to a simmer. Simmer gently 4 hours, stirring occasionally. While hot, pack into hot sterilized 1-quart canning jars, leaving about 1/8 inch headspace. Run a narrow spatula down between mincemeat and side of jar to release any air. Top with sterilized lids; firmly screw on bands. Place in a draft-free area to cool. Store in a cool, dry place. Makes 7 quarts.

Mincemeat, a staple in the English pantry, makes a welcome gift. This recipe, redolent of spices and brandy, is one of the best.

Lemon Curd

Grated peel of 4 lemons
Juice of 4 lemons (about 1 cup)
4 eggs, beaten
1/2 cup butter, cut in small pieces
2 cups sugar

Lemon curd, sometimes called lemon cheese, is a very common English preserve. It's used as a spread for sandwiches, muffins, crumpets and so forth, and also makes a delicious tart filling. Lemon curd doesn't keep indefinitely so make only as much as you will use in a couple of weeks.

In the top of a large double boiler, combine lemon peel, lemon juice, eggs, butter and sugar. Place over simmering water and stir until sugar is dissolved. Continue to cook, stirring occasionally, until thickened and smooth. While hot, pour into hot sterilized 1/2-pint canning jars, leaving about 1/8 inch headspace. Run a narrow spatula down between lemon curd and side of jar to release air. Top with sterilized lids; firmly screw on bands. Place in a draft-free area to cool. Store in a cool, dry place. Makes about 1 pint.

Raspberry Jam

3 pounds (6 cups) sugar
**2-1/2 pounds fresh
raspberries, rinsed**

*Raspberry jam is used in many tea recipes. Why not try a homemade batch?
This recipe produces a fairly soft jam that's good for spreading. Be sure to
weigh the raspberries in the grocery store or at home—it is important to get
the correct ratio of raspberries to sugar.*

Preheat oven to 100F (40C), then turn it off. Pour sugar into a
large ovenproof bowl and set in oven to warm slightly (do not allow
sugar to melt). Put raspberries in a large saucepan or preserving kettle
and cook over low heat until berries begin to release juice. Increase heat
and boil gently 10 minutes. Add warmed sugar and stir until sugar is
dissolved. Return to a boil; boil rapidly 2 minutes. Pour jam into hot
sterilized 1/2-pint canning jars, leaving about 1/8 inch headspace. Run a
narrow spatula down between jam and side of jar to release air. Top
with sterilized lids; firmly screw on bands. Place in a draft-free area to
cool. Store in a cool, dry area. Makes about 3 pints.

Strawberry Conserve

6 cups sugar
2 cups water
**1-1/2 quarts (6 cups) fresh
strawberries, washed,
hulled**

*This very old recipe gives a conserve with a wonderful texture. It's delicious
with freshly baked scones.*

Measure 2 cups of the sugar into a large saucepan or preserving
kettle. Add water. Stir over low heat until sugar is dissolved, then
increase heat and bring syrup to a boil. Boil 15 minutes, stirring occasionally. Add 2 cups strawberries and boil 15 minutes longer, stirring
occasionally. Stir in 2 cups more sugar and 2 cups more strawberries
and boil 15 minutes longer, stirring occasionally. Stir in remaining 2
cups sugar and 2 cups strawberries and boil 15 minutes longer, stirring
occasionally. Pour into shallow pans. Cover lightly with a clean cloth
and let stand at room temperature overnight. The syrup will thicken
and the berries will become plump. Pack into hot sterilized 1/2-pint
canning jars and seal. Makes about 3 pints.

Source Directory

Should you live in an area where good teas are not available, you can mail-order them from the following companies. Many of these sources also carry gourmet preserves or other specialties that will make your afternoon tea party authentic and delicious. Call or write for further information or a catalog.

Tea Importers, Inc.
47 Riverside Avenue
Westport, Connecticut 06880
(203) 226-3301

Community Kitchens
P.O. Box 3778
Baton Rouge, Louisiana 70821
(800) 535-9901

J & K Trading Company
10808 Garland Drive
Culver City, California 90230
(213) 836-3334

Simpson & Vail, Inc.
P.O. Box 309
Pleasantville, New York 10570
(914) 747-1336

Crabtree & Evelyn, Ltd.
P.O. Box 167
Woodstock, Connecticut 06281
(203) 928-2766

The Grace Tea Company, Ltd.
50 W. 17th Street
New York, New York 10011
(212) 255-2935

Metric Chart

Comparison to Metric Measure

When You Know	Symbol	Multiply By	To Find	Symbol
teaspoons	tsp	5.0	milliliters	ml
tablespoons	tbsp	15.0	milliliters	ml
fluid ounces	fl. oz.	30.0	milliliters	ml
cups	c	0.24	liters	l
pints	pt.	0.47	liters	l

When You Know	Symbol	Multiply By	To Find	Symbol
quarts	qt.	0.95	liters	l
ounces	oz.	28.0	grams	g
pounds	lb.	0.45	kilograms	kg
Fahrenheit	F	5/9 (after subtracting 32)	Celsius	C

Fahrenheit to Celsius

F	C
200—205	95
220—225	105
245—250	120
275	135
300—305	150
325—330	165
345—350	175
370—375	190
400—405	205
425—430	220
445—450	230
470—475	245
500	260

Liquid Measure to Liters

1/4 cup	=	0.06 liters
1/2 cup	=	0.12 liters
3/4 cup	=	0.18 liters
1 cup	=	0.24 liters
1-1/4 cups	=	0.3 liters
1-1/2 cups	=	0.36 liters
2 cups	=	0.48 liters
2-1/2 cups	=	0.6 liters
3 cups	=	0.72 liters
3-1/2 cups	=	0.84 liters
4 cups	=	0.96 liters
4-1/2 cups	=	1.08 liters
5 cups	=	1.2 liters
5-1/2 cups	=	1.32 liters

Liquid Measure to Milliliters

1/4 teaspoon	=	1.25 milliliters
1/2 teaspoon	=	2.5 milliliters
3/4 teaspoon	=	3.75 milliliters
1 teaspoon	=	5.0 milliliters
1-1/4 teaspoons	=	6.25 milliliters
1-1/2 teaspoons	=	7.5 milliliters
1-3/4 teaspoons	=	8.75 milliliters
2 teaspoons	=	10.0 milliliters
1 tablespoon	=	15.0 milliliters
2 tablespoons	=	30.0 milliliters

Index